FORESIGHT IS 20/20

FORESIGHT IS 20/20

8 STRATEGIES FOR SUCCESS TO OVERCOME OBSTACLES

MICHAEL WARNER, ED.D

Copyright © 2021 by Michael Warner
Foresight is 20/20:
8 Strategies for Success to Overcome Obstacles

All rights reserved. No part of this publication may be reproduced, distributed or transmitted in any form or by any means, including photocopying, recording, or other electronic or mechanical methods, without the prior written permission of the publisher, except in the case of brief quotations embodied in critical reviews and certain other noncommercial uses permitted by copyright law.

Although the author and publisher have made every effort to ensure that the information in this book was correct at press time, the author and publisher do not assume and hereby disclaim any liability to any party for any loss, damage, or disruption caused by errors or omissions, whether such errors or omissions result from negligence, accident, or any other cause.

Adherence to all applicable laws and regulations, including international, federal, state and local governing professional licensing, business practices, advertising, and all other aspects of doing business in the US, Canada or any other jurisdiction is the sole responsibility of the reader and consumer.

Neither the author nor the publisher assumes any responsibility or liability whatsoever on behalf of the consumer or reader of this material. Any perceived slight of any individual or organization is purely unintentional.

The resources in this book are provided for informational purposes only and should not be used to replace the specialized training and professional judgment of a health care or mental health care professional.

Neither the author nor the publisher can be held responsible for the use of the information provided within this book. Please always consult a trained professional before making any decision regarding treatment of yourself or others.

ISBN:
978-1-7368624-0-7 (Paperback)
978-1-7368624-2-1 (Hardcover)

DOWNLOAD YOUR FREE WORKBOOK

As a gift to my readers to help you get the most out of this book, I encourage you to download a **FREE WORKBOOK** to use alongside this book.

GO TO
WWW.SUMMITPERFORMANCESOLUTIONSLLC.COM
TO DOWNLOAD TODAY!

Summit Performance Solutions, llc

Website: www.summitperformancesolutionsllc.com
Email: michael@summitperformancesolutionsllc.com

DEDICATION

This book is dedicated to my beautiful wife and my two amazing boys, who always know when Daddy is working but still decide to come say hello and see if I need anything. Lindsey, thank you for always supporting me through this time-consuming endeavor and leaving me little notes telling me not to work too hard or stay up too late. I truly could not have completed this without the love and understanding you show me day in and day out, as we both know I burn the candle at both ends and am always looking for what's next. The completion of this book is just as much yours as it is mine; you have been with me every step of the way, providing me with the support and love needed to complete this milestone. Thank you from the bottom of my heart. I love you more than anything, my love.

I would also like to dedicate this book to my father. He is not around to see me complete this momentous accomplishment in my life, but I hope he knows that the drive and motivation he instilled in me throughout my life is part of the reason why I chose to write this book. Thank you, Dad, for always pushing me in my life to be better but never making me feel like I am not enough. I hope I am instilling the same sense of drive and motivation in my boys but also making them feel as safe and supported as you did me. Thanks, Pop, for always being there for me when I needed you, as I would not be at this point in my life if it weren't for your many lectures about the importance of education, development, and advancement in all we do. I love you, Dad, and we miss you every day.

There is one quality that one must possess to win, and that is definiteness of purpose, the knowledge of what one wants, and a burning desire to possess it.

- Napoleon Hill

TABLE OF CONTENTS

DEDICATION

INTRODUCTION — 1

CHAPTER ONE — 9
Life is a Complex System

CHAPTER TWO — 21
Life Can be Dry at Times

CHAPTER THREE — 41
Trust the Process

CHAPTER FOUR — 57
Teachable Moments

CHAPTER FIVE — 71
Rinse and Repeat

CHAPTER SIX — 87
It's Human Nature

CHAPTER SEVEN — 107
Practice Makes Potential

CHAPTER EIGHT	123
Thanks for the Feedback!	
CHAPTER NINE	139
This is Only a Test...	
CHAPTER TEN	155
The Solution Isn't Always Simple	
CHAPTER ELEVEN	173
A Different Type of Transition Blanket	
CHAPTER TWELVE	191
The Bumps are What We Climb On	
CHAPTER THIRTEEN	207
Life is Like a Road...To Anywhere	
CHAPTER FOURTEEN	223
Next Stop...	
CONCLUSION	237

INTRODUCTION

Have you ever been exposed to something in your life that changed the way you look at adversity or challenges? Something that really made a difference in the way you perceive something? Think about a time in your life when you approached an obstacle or barrier and wished you had the tools to work through the process and push past it. I know have encountered many transition points in my life where I wish I had a process available to me to push through the obstacles and barriers that we encounter.

Let me begin by providing a little background on why I chose to write this book in the first place. About two years ago, I read a book that changed my perspective. Some of you may be familiar with it—it is titled *Can't Hurt Me* by David Goggins. If you have not read this book, you need to. I read it and was motivated in a way that continues to guide me during the many transitions of my life and the barriers and obstacles I face along the way. One of the things Goggins discusses is taking risks to obtain what you want as you work through the many transitions in your life. I am paraphrasing, but the idea is that if you want something bad enough, then you need to take risks and work hard. Anyone who is familiar with Goggins book knows the struggles he has dealt with, and I am still very impressed with how he has succeeded and continues to succeed. (Also, we had the same job in the USAF, so much respect to my fellow TACP.) The reason I bring this up is because it sparked a desire in me to live up to my potential and succeed.

    This book is based on a process that I developed while completing my doctorate degree. It is called the Transitional Learning Process (refered to in this book as the TLP), and it is a process of Eight Strategies for Success that were created to help work through the different obstacles and barriers associated with life's transitions. This is a self-help book, not a textbook. Life is full of transition points, and at each transition point we have a choice. Each strategy builds on those previous and shows how—when we remain positive and confident and live up to our potential—success is possible and for the taking. The great thing about this process is that it can be applied to everyday life and the many different transitions we encounter. The

TLP works within a given system. Life is a system—a complex system that changes with each transition. You will see through the examples, experiences and stories provided, that when the strategies for success are applied to the numerous transitions in our complex system of life, success is possible.

The road to success relies on our perception of potential and on our abilities. Anything can be accomplished if we break things down into manageable steps. The TLP is a sequential process for success that, when applied, can be extremely beneficial. This book will guide you through the many experiences of my life where the TLP strategies were applied in some form or fashion (including writing this book and my current situation). As the TLP is sequential, so are the examples, each building on another starting from childhood and proceeding throughout my life, helping you see just how beneficial the process can be. Life is complex, and each of us deals with the many transitions in our own way. The obstacles and barriers we face are specific to our own journey, and it is up to us to make the choices that benefit our own situation. Sometimes it is clear, and sometimes it is not. If I have learned anything from my own experiences, it is that we have no idea what is next; we can only take each encounter as it comes and address each obstacle or barrier as it approaches.

I was once told that life is full of processes—a complex system filled with steps for success. As long as we break things down into manageable steps, we should be able to accomplish anything and be successful. Within this complex system we experience different processes, different transitions, and different points of learning. There are different times in our lives when we encounter continuous learning experiences that help us transition to our next learning experience. We have two choices—we can either embrace the learning activity we encounter or we can deny it and continue on the path that we're currently on. I have always felt it beneficial to embrace these different learning or continuous learning points, and this book is meant to do just that.

As a member of the military and somebody who has followed structure and systematic thinking throughout his career, I can say that the process presented truly works when applied to the proper situation. The contents of this book utilize a combination of academic terms, theories, personal experiences, and examples to present the process. Did I forget to mention humor, as I feel laughter is always the best and only medicine? As an avid reader, I love reading content that really puts me in the situation. Content that really helps me understand what the author is trying to portray. Isn't this one of the reasons why we read? So we can better equip ourselves to understand different things and move through life, the complex system that we all engage in, with as much success as possible? One thing I try to make sure of for my boys—I have two of them, five and eight—is that they learn to become an expert at one thing: their own life and potential.

Life is a continuous process; it is filled with different transitions, experiences, and points when we have to look at the situation in different ways and apply different strategies or processes. I have been a member of the military and have worked in public service for the government for over twenty years. I have experienced so many things in my life and my career that can't be explained by this book—or with words—but what I can do is provide insight into how I dealt with some of the many transitions and how I applied the different strategies for success within the TLP to these situations. I stated earlier that the point of this book is to help the reader understand life's transitions, understand how these strategies for success can help us get through our complex system of life, and understand the different barriers and obstacles we face on a daily basis.

We have all encountered obstacles and barriers, questioning what the next steps are. I cannot say it enough: we are experts at one thing and that is our own life. We know what works best for us; we know the things that help us move through these different transition points in our own lives. I have worked through these transitions by applying the concepts within the numerous strategies for success present within transitional learning. Now, this isn't to say that if you apply these strategies you'll be able to rule the world or get through anything that you encounter. What it's meant to do is help you through your own transitions and show you how each strategy can be applied and can be successful. As a member of the United States Air Force, I have served on active duty, in the Air National Guard, and the Air Force Reserves. During this time I have served both in peacetime and combat operations, served overseas, and served in numerous training and instructor roles. We all learn in different ways, and we all encounter different transitions throughout our lives.

During my doctoral studies I completed a capstone project that focused on transitional learning, where I developed the Transitional Learning Process (TLP). The TLP is described in more detail in the following chapters, but it is based on a system-thinking approach while applying performance-improvement strategies to the current obstacles or barriers we may encounter—in our professional or academic lives, or in life in general. That is the beauty of this process and, in my opinion, the most intriguing aspect of this book.

This book will not only provide you with the strategies for success, but it will also provide you with specific personal experiences and examples from my own life where applying the concepts within the strategies for success has really been successful. I am a visual, hands-on learner. Maybe it's because of my military background and the way that I have been taught in my life, but I learn best when I can see it, when I can touch it, when I can visualize it, but most importantly—relate to it. That is the beauty of what this book portrays. It will truly show you how each strategy can be applied and put you into the situation where you can see just how effective and successful you can be when applying the Eight Strategies for Success within the TLP.

So, let's set out on this journey together and see how the TLP and its strategies for success have benefited my life and can make a difference in yours. I promise you will not be disappointed. Trust the process, and it will show you how success is possible. Foresight is twenty-twenty when we apply the TLP. Let me prove it to you. Dig in, and let's get started

CHAPTER ONE

Life is a Complex System

So what is a transition? The Merriam-Webster definition of a transition is, basically, the process or a period of changing from one state or condition to another. I don't really understand what that means, do you? Simply put, a transition (as I define it for this book) is when we move from one point in our life to another, whether physically, mentally, emotionally, spiritually, or something to that effect. The best part of life's transitions is that they are continuously happening as we move through our lives, through our personal complex system. In education, we see transitional learning mainly through the three primary transitions in our academic career. This is from elementary to middle school, from middle school to high school, and then from high school to college. Within these three transitions we experience different levels of understanding and different levels of comprehension, but it's not all academic. We can all attest to the fact that during our K-12 years we deal with transitions that extend from the classroom. We deal with emotionally, physically, and mentally based transitions as well as academic transitions. We are transitioning every day as we are growing within this time. We also know that transitioning students often experience significant academic, social, emotional, physical, and developmental changes that may affect their performance, reactions, character, and overall persona.

I'm a very dedicated and involved father, and I spend the majority of my time focusing on my family and the things that need to be done within my household. So, it's very interesting to see the different transitions in my own life, whether it's within my household for my children, within my marriage, or within my professional career, and try to figure out the best way to apply the proper solutions to these transitions. I tell my wife she has the hardest job in the world, which is caring for our children and taking care of our household. I appreciate what she does more than words can explain, and I know it's not always easy. She is dealing with numerous transitions of her own on an everyday basis. Not only does she experience the transitions of our young children, she also experiences the challenges of our older children—as I have two stepchildren on the brink of young adulthood. They are dealing with their own set of transitions. I give her all the credit in the world and commend her for the amazing job she does while still helping me.

Adult learners move differently through transitional learning than adolescent learners. Adolescents mainly deal with the three primary transitions that get them to college. Adult learners are at a point where they are focusing more on moving from one organization to another or from one position to another as an employee in their current career. As an adult, I moved from military service to government service. There are always different transitions that adult learners may face when they are moving through different points of their life, i.e., moving through their complex system. The consistent factor present in all these situations is the idea that this complex system of life is a process of manageable steps for success that never go astray—as long as we break challenges into these manageable steps, and we attack these situations, barriers, and obstacles with this in mind, success is very possible. That's what the TLP does—it helps the learner, the child, the adult, the individual, who is applying these different strategies for success, get through the difficulties they face within their transitions.

I want to provide you with an incident in my life where transitional learning was present. As it happens with many young people, I did not always make the best decisions when I was growing up. I did OK in school, receiving decent grades. I worked, played sports, and I listened to my parents (when I felt like it). Overall, I was a good kid, and I did the right thing. I'm not going to say that there weren't times when I could have made better choices—times when I was going through different transitions within my own journey and in my own complex system of life. My parents divorced when I was twelve years old, but I maintained a relationship with both of them and spent time living with my mom and with my dad. I'm not going to say it was the easiest transition, but that's something we'll get into later in the book. So, to kick this off, let's provide a little bit of humor: a situation or story that maybe some of you can relate to but where all of you can see where transitional learning was present.

After I graduated from high school, I headed to college. In high school, I was a good B student, but I know I could have applied myself more. I was a student-athlete. I ran track and field and played football. I was also on the swim team and raised with a Catholic school education. My focus in high school was on sports. I worked, I went to school, and I played sports.

I did socialize as well. I went to parties, hung out, went to the mall, and did all the things that teenagers do, but my main focus was on sports, work, and school. This comes from my dad's influential, hard-working demeanor. My dad was an amazing man. He showed me how to respect, how to love, how to be compassionate, how to be understanding, and how to apply myself. This is why my wife tells me I burn the candle at both ends and always have a plan A, B, and C. He provided me with all the morals and character traits that most people would expect, but (just as many of us do) I made mistakes.

I did not have my first sip of alcohol until after I graduated high school, so when I went to college—let's just say I experienced it with no regrets. There was one instance when I was nineteen years old and home from college on a break. My stepmother was out of town visiting family, and it was just me, my father, and my stepbrother, who is a year older than me. I stated earlier that my father was an amazing man. He was very fair and understanding and, as he knew that I was a young adult moving through these different transitions of our complex system of life, he tried to work with me so we both felt comfortable in our situation. He had one rule: he told me that if I was going to stay out any later than 3:00 a.m. I needed to stay at a friend's house. He did not want me coming in the house after 3:00 a.m.—especially if I had been drinking with friends. So, of course, just like many nineteen-year-old young adults, I thought I was smarter than my dad. I thought that if I came home at 3:00 a.m., and told him I was home, I could sneak back out, come back with my friends at 5:00 a.m., and he would never know the difference. So, that's just what I did. I played it up pretty good too when I went in at 3:00 a.m. and told him I was home. He wasn't too happy to be woken up at three o'clock, but he mumbled something and rolled back over. I thought it was smooth sailing after that. I thought I'd sneak right back out of the house, and he would never know the difference. He would be up in two hours to go to work at five, and I could stay out all night partying and hanging out and have a good time. Then I could bring my friends back at five o'clock to continue the party. Brilliant idea.

This is where transitional learning plays a role in decisions. After I snuck back out, I went to a place where all my friends were still gathered. They commended me on my covert return, and the party continued. I wanted to be the cool friend and say, "Hey, let's keep the party going. My dad goes to work at five, and my stepmother is away. There's nobody home. We can just go hang out at my house." In my mind, I thought this was a fantastic idea, and there was no way I was going to get in trouble or get caught. We finished up where we were, and at about 4:45 a.m. we took taxis (this was before the days of Uber and Lyft) and headed back towards my neighborhood.

Let me paint the picture for you of the environment where I grew up in Staten Island, New York. Picture a residential suburban neighborhood, a middle-class family size, and a ranch-style house. We lived on a corner lot. My idea was that we would go around the corner by my house and hang out there until after five when my dad went to work. Then we would go in my house and keep it going. Simple enough, right? The thing that I did not take into account was the fact that we all had been drinking and probably weren't in the best state of mind. We were not being quiet, so it didn't dawn on us that every single person in the vicinity of my house could probably hear us on the corner, including my dad. Much to my surprise, my father walked around the corner to find me and all my friends hanging out, laughing, and joking. He looked right in my face, pointed his finger, and told me to come here.

I didn't think I was doing anything wrong at that point, so I strolled over to him without a care in the world. Was it the alcohol, or the fact that I had this great idea, or the fact that I knew everything? Who knows, but I was quickly going to learn. My father brought me into the house and began to provide me with one of his detailed, experienced, very long lectures. There were two things growing up that we could always count on when it came to my dad: that any time he got mad his neck jowls would fluctuate, and he would get red, and second, that we were going to get a long-winded, full-of-experience lecture when we screwed up. On this occasion, we went in the house into the kitchen, and my dad continued to provide me with one of his very insightful, very detailed lectures on respect and the rules. I felt it would be beneficial to tell him to relax. I was in a state of mind that is termed *beer muscles or liquid courage*. As I said earlier, we had been drinking and having a good time, so I thought it would be appropriate to tell my father, with my hot, smelly alcohol breath, "Yo bro, chill."

Let me be honest on his actual response and paint the picture for you in this transitional learning moment. My father was one of the sweetest, most understanding, compassionate, and funniest people I have ever met in my entire life. His presence brought happiness to everybody he was around just because of the kind of person he was. Yes, he would get upset, and his jowls would flare, but 95 percent of the time my father was the nicest, funniest, happiest person you could meet. This was not the case at 5:00 a.m. on a Tuesday morning, when he was leaving for work and his nineteen-year-old son decided to breathe hot alcohol breath in his face and say, "Yo bro, chill." My father's forms of discipline, back in the 1980s when I was a child growing up, were lectures, taking things away, and sending us to our rooms. I'm not going to say we didn't get our hair pulled by Mom in the store once in a while, or get the belt or a spanking, but all in all that was not the type of discipline my parents portrayed to us children. My grandmother, God rest her soul, liked the wooden spoon and the broom handle. But, see, at this point, I was nineteen years old. I was not a child. I was an adult with an adult mind and an adult way of thinking, and most of all—could face adult consequences. My father was very big on respect. Trust me, I heard about it in the many, many, many lectures I have received in my lifetime. Needless to say, he was pretty upset about my comment, as it was very disrespectful.

After the smelly alcohol breath settled and the anger settled in, my father—without hesitation—pulled back his arm and hand and provided me with a shot to the jaw that sent me to the ground. Now I do not condone violence. I make sure my kids understand that we keep our hands to ourselves, and we deal with things in better ways, but let's be honest, I deserved it. I was on the floor looking up in dismay that my father just planted me. My father helped me up, brought me to my room, took my boots off, and even provided my friends with a story that did not make me look bad. This is the kind of man he was.

Let's fast-forward to when I woke up to reality at about 2:00 p.m., sober, with a clear mind and a full understanding of the situation. I was terrified. You know how we always say hindsight is twenty-twenty? Don't we wish foresight were twenty-twenty, as the title of this book illuminates? I had plenty of time to reflect on what had happened before my father got home from work at about 4:30 p.m. We had a finished basement in my house in Staten Island, and that's where I spent most of my recovery time after an exciting night. As I sat on the couch in my basement, watching TV and thinking about what had happened—I was shitting in my pants. In my mind, I was a toast.

It was 4:32 p.m. when I heard the door open upstairs. I remember looking at the digital clock on the cable box. I could hear my father's work boots on the floor and with every step a sense of fear (that only somebody in this type of situation can relate to) came over me. With every step through the living room, the fear just heightened and heightened, anxiety just built and built—until he opened the door and took two steps down the stairs. Now, I don't know if he could really see the fear on my face, or if he thought it was a good teaching moment, or if he just felt really bad about laying me out, but his reaction was something that I was not expecting. He simply looked at me and said, "Yo bro, chill. What the fuck is wrong with you?"

I didn't have an answer, as I knew it was not the smartest decision. My father just chuckled and shook his head and said to me, "Don't ever come into this house like that again or speak to me like that again." I felt a huge weight just lift off my shoulders. I'm sure it was something that my father could see; we had a nice conversation, with no lecture, after that. My father talked to me in a different way than he'd ever spoken to me before. He talked to me as an adult, as somebody who has transitioned from an adolescent into a young adult. My father talked to me about decisions he made in his life that he wished he could take back, about things that he did, ways he reacted to his father who taught him—hey, this is probably not the right thing to do. He helped me understand that we all make mistakes and that we all do things that we wish we could take back, but we learn from them and move on. It was very relatable and something that I truly embraced and understood.

This is an example of transitional learning. My father is no longer with us, and I feel a hole in my heart every day without his presence, but I know he still watches down on me and hopes I make good choices when transitions occur; I am sure he would love to give me a lecture when I don't. When we go through these different transitions in our lives, we look at these experiences, and we learn from them. Our complex system of life continues to provide us with learning opportunities, so the next time we do not make the best choice, we can learn from these events and be better for them. It's not always going to be a situation where maybe you're doing something inappropriate or incorrect. It could just be an instance when you approach a barrier or an obstacle that you're having difficulty breaking through or getting to the other side of. This can be very frustrating; it can hurt your confidence, and it can make you question things, but we have to remember—in this complex system of life—these transitions are normal. As a society, we can all admit that my response and reaction in this situation was completely inappropriate and incorrect. My dad took this opportunity to make it a learning moment, to help me understand that life is a learning process and that we all deal with things and have to work through them. This is what this book is meant to do: help the reader understand and relate to the situation and the transitions we face in our complex system of life and see how the strategies can be applied and be successful.

In the next chapter, we will dive into issues with learning, systematic thinking, the components of Performance Improvement, and transitional learning—and how that relates to the TLP and ideas surrounding this book.

CHAPTER TWO

Life Can be Dry at Times

Life is full of transitions within the learning process, times when we hit barriers and obstacles within our complex system. These issues can be anything from life, to school, to work, to relationships, and so on. Some examples would be your understanding and comprehension of things you learn in school and what you learn at work, issues with the things you're supposed to do in life, and the cognitive functions in your mind affecting how you perceive things. This includes your emotions—only you know how you deal with these different transitions. Perception by you and by others is a large part of what we see within our complex system of life. We worry about what other people think, what other people see, and how other people see us. We worry about how we're perceived—whether it's in our household, in school, in our job, or in society as a whole. These are all things we think about, contemplate, and reflect on—what we question about ourselves and others.

The questions and perceptions that we think about are what hinders us sometimes while moving through the different transitions of life. Think about an instance when you are at work or in a job where you don't get along with the people you work with. There's one person in particular that you feel does not necessarily like you, and you think he or she has it out for you. Unless you approach this transition with an open mind, this perception is going to be what you think is reality. You have a choice. You can go in the direction of approaching this individual and trying to speak with them or you can continue down the avenue of your own perception and not engage. Which direction do you think is going to be most beneficial for you and your life? The better option would be to engage and try and resolve the issue and overcome the barrier. This increases the chances for a successful relationship in the future and adjusts your perception into reality, as now you know the truth. This is just an example, but it shows how we can transition and learn from this transition. We see it in our own work, we see it in our emotions, we see it in the way we comprehend things. The choice is simple, in the sense that we can choose one of two directions. We can either deal with the obstacle or the barrier within the transition or we don't deal with it. I'm not going to say there isn't a gray area in the sense of the way things go within our complex system of life, because we all know there is, but we can either deal with these issues and barriers or we can choose not to, and that is the simple fact.

I joined the military when I was twenty-one years old. I had originally attended college for about three years and received a whopping forty-five credits. I was in an unsanctioned fraternity, partying and drinking six nights a week, with school being the last priority on my mind. I had already failed-out once and had to go to community college to be readmitted. Obviously, I was not on the right track. My father and I knew I needed a change and after watching *G.I. Jane* numerous times, I decided to contact a recruiter and eventually join the military. I know it seems odd, but for some reason that movie had a huge impact on me reaching out to a recruiter and joining the military.

I spoke with every recruiter out there and decided on the Unites States Air Force (USAF). I wanted to leave for basic training as soon as possible, so my recruiter sold me on the idea of going in the Open-General occupation field. Those in the USAF know what that means. Well, I did not at the time, and my recruiter informed me that my scores were really good and that Open-General meant I could have any job in that category when I got to basic training. He did not tell me it meant I would be placed in a career field of the Air Force's choosing, based on what the USAF needed to fill at that time.. Most likely, it would be the Services or Security Forces career field. During the time I attended basic training, new recruits were able to volunteer for career fields that fell within Air Force Special Operations Command (AFSOC). (Yes, they have one.) I took all the physical entry tests, listened to all the recruiters, and chose Tactical Air Command and Control Party (TACP). Simply put, we travel with and support the Army during ground operations and assist them with Air coverage, calling in Airstrikes when required. We control what's called close air support (CAS) missions in support of our aligned Army unit. How could you not choose this when the recruiter comes into your flight with a sick, crisp black berete with a huge dip, shows a video of blowing shit up, and then ends his speech with, "Who likes drinking beers and dropping bombs?" I was sold.

I finished basic training and headed to Hurlburt Field, Florida, for training to become a TACP. This is where perception and the chance to make a choice come into play. After arriving at the schoolhouse, I was told the next class would not begin for a few weeks, so we would be on Awaiting Further Instructions (AFI) until then. This meant a lot of cleaning the dorm. It also gave us a chance to interact with current students in the program and get some insight. This was in the year 2000, and the washout rate was pretty high during this time—about 50 percent of the students made it through without being recycled back.

I began questioning my own abilities. This had a lot to do with struggles of insecurity I had faced as a child, which you will see in later stories throughout the book. I began losing myself in my own perceptions and started to question everything. I even started trying to figure out ways of getting out of there and either going home or getting a different job. I am not proud of it, but I mentally began to give up. It wasn't until I received a call from one of the many recruiters I spoke with during my journey to enlistment that everything changed. He told me that we all have a choice: to push forward or step back. If we push forward and give it everything, we know we tried and can be satisfied with our attempt. If we step back, we will never know our true potential, and utlimately believe our incorrect perceptions.

He was right, what was I doing? The worst that could happen was I wouldn't make it, but at least I would have tried my best and lived up to my full potential at that time. Long story short, I completed the training without being recycled and enjoyed a memorable, exciting twelve-year career as a TACP, deploying on numerous occasions, helping train new controllers, and forming bonds that I still have today (miss ya, graybush and mini-me). It wasn't until my body started falling apart, and my wife had to rub my entire body with icy hot that I knew I needed to hang up the black beret and move on. It was all due to a choice. What if I didn't make that choice? Where would I be now? Who knows, but what I do know is, I wouldn't change it for the world. (Thanks to TSgt Castillo—hope you are enjoying retirement.)

Just as with many things, there is a dry and academic-based background component to the TLP, as there are different aspects that were used to build the process and the Eight Strategies for Success. With my background in the military and government service, you can imagine structure is a primary aspect of my life. My complex system focuses a lot on systems thinking, which views everything as a process. I truly believe that as long as we break things down into manageable steps, we can accomplish anything.

I like to follow a system. I like structure and enjoy creating and developing curriculum, where I can provide instruction to members of the military and the government. The TLP was developed from within the field of performance improvement (PI), specifically the theories of Human Performance Improvement (HPI), and it combines models and terms associated with PI and systems thinking to create a process of strategies for success that, when followed sequentially, can build confidence. It can assist in accomplishing the task at hand and help push through the barrier or obstacle with a systems thinking mindset. Of course, I have to give some background information on the concepts, theories, and models that are associated with the TLP and its creation. I promise I will try not bore you with this content and most of it will be provided in this chapter to give a breakdown on the framework of the TLP.

HPI is a form of organizational development that focuses on increasing output and improving efficiency for a particular process or procedure at different points in our journey. It is the study and practice of improving this productivity within your complex system by designing and developing effective interventions and results-oriented comprehensive and systematic decisions. HPI differs from training in that you cast a wider net because our complex system has wide ranges; it's not a specific point A to point B. HPI recognizes that there are performance issues due to barriers and obstacles you may be facing within your transition periods. This might be the reason why you're not meeting your performance goals. Performance goals don't have to be academic or professionally driven; they can be goals that you're trying to set in your life. An example that is very important to me is parenting—my boys are five and eight years old. My wife and I have developed a goal chart for them, and there are eight to ten items that we have written down for them. Those items are their goals for the week. I'm all about providing contingent rewards and providing motivation to assist them move through their transitions, but I also don't want them to think that in order to have a successful week, they need to obtain something to be rewarded. As long as they accomplish their goals, they have been successful. So, we developed this list of goals for the week so that their primary benefit is accomplishing all their goals, and if they accomplish all of their goals for the week by making good choices and working through their transitions, that is the primary reward.

I admit, because they are little and we're helping them understand the benefit of accomplishing your goals and receiving something in return, whether it's something material or something within yourself, we do tell them, "If you accomplish all your goals there may be a contingent reward." In this sense, a contingent reward is getting to play outside and no schoolwork all weekend or they don't have to review what they did for the week. These are different benefits and rewards that don't necessarily mean a toy or a trip to McDonald's, which they do get as well, sometimes. The main point is, we're helping them understand that if you set these attainable goals for the week, and then you accomplish these goals, the primary reward is just as much within yourself as it is something external. When you meet your performance goals you're building your own confidence, whether you know it or not.

HPI is where the systems aspect comes in. This is where you look at the analysis, the interventions, the implementation, and the evaluation of the different performance-improvement directions you're considering. This is not the premise of this book. This book is not meant to lay out specific theories and ideas and provide you with academic content you can apply to a paper or project. It's not a textbook. The point I want to make in regards to HPI is that it's a systematic process that involves systems thinking, which indicates we all work within a process. Like I've said many times to this point, we live in a complex system, and if we break our transitions into manageable steps, we can accomplish anything and be successful.

Systems thinking implements the idea that everything works within a specified system and that everything is a process within that given system—the complex system of life that we've already touched upon. This idea presents itself in some form or fashion within any organization, agency, academic setting, or simply within the different aspects of life. According to James A. Pershing's *Handbook of Human Performance Technology*,[1] this definition is used mainly in the pro-

---

1   James Pershing, "Human Performance Technology Fundamentals," in *Handbook of Human Performance Technology: Principles, Practices, and Potential*, 3rd Ed. (San Francisco: John Wiley & Sons, Inc, 2006), 5-34.

fessional setting, but the concepts of it can be applied to any specific setting in the complex system of life that we live in. Performance Management (PM), a branch of HPI, has six specific steps towards success. These steps include:

- planning
- monitoring
- developing strategies
- improving on those strategies
- measuring those strategies
- repeating the ones that are beneficial and successful in our PM plan

The point I am getting at is that when it comes to HPI and PM, there is a continuous improvement process where the overall goal is quality, right? We're trying to be successful in our transitions and be as effective and efficient as we can. You know the saying: quality over quantity. There are four main concepts that we look at within continuous improvement. They are:

- commitment
- strategy
- process
- performance

This is all within the continuous learning-improvement process we encounter daily. *Commitment* looks at compelling awareness and shared goals. *Strategy* is your vision, your mission, and the different deliverables that you're going to have within that strategy. *Process* helps you map the process, and it assists with analysis, as it will focus on all the different aspects within the chosen process. The performance aspect measures your performance and your management procedures—all for the goal of the most effective and efficient product, the quality so to speak. The process is meant to assist in mitigating issues and concerns logically. It is also meant to introduce methods for enhanced collaboration and teamwork, whether at work or within personal life. To that end, it provides strategies for understanding and processing feedback, which is vital for successful thinking. The TLP can assist with increasing confidence and knowledge through the establishment of individual performance goals. The TLP looks to institute problem-solving techniques to address organizational and individual barriers that we all face within our complex system. It provides strategies for individual success within time management and the ability to maintain a schedule. The process can assist with accomplishing job-related tasks through the use of an individual performance plan. Finally, it can show you how working through these different transitions by applying the strategies for success can help us be better and progress through the complex system we all encounter in life. Now, that's a lot to digest, but don't worry, we'll do it in parts, and you'll see what I mean. Remember, it's a process!

Personally, I would rather make sure I'm accomplishing my tasks, my requirements, my duties in the best way possible instead of for the most possible output, quality over quantity. I created the TLP and its Eight Strategies for Success through my academic research while completing my doctorate degree—with the idea of creating a Transitional Learning Process which can guide us, lead us, and show us that victory, our own championship within our complex system of life, is possible.

The TLP was created through ideas and concepts associated with HPI and systems thinking. The primary goal of the TLP is to assist us in functioning more effectively, building confidence, increasing our overall understanding of the issue, obstacle, and related tasks that we're trying to accomplish—and ultimately be successful. When implemented in order, the Eight Strategies for Success created within the TLP can assist in the advancement of your learning, performance, and development within life's transitions, and help you be successful when you apply yourself and live up to your true potential. The TLP is based on a systematic thinking approach, which applies PI-based strategies, to an obstacle or barrier you may be facing within your chosen transition. The TLP formula for success combines the concepts of PI models—such as the cognitive approach and strategic-impact planning—with general systems theory, or systems thinking, to create the Eight Strategies for Success. The TLP looks to help improve our abilities to work through life's transitions, so we can become more efficient, effective, build confidence, and increase our overall understanding and reaction to the obstacle or barrier we are currently facing. These system processes can be anything from our job to school to relationships to everyday activities. By applying what we know, and working through the system in place, we can use the TLP to get us through and approach the next level. It can provide positive feedback, demonstrate knowledge, build positive relationships, enhance collaboration and teamwork, instill confidence, and help us ultimately succeed.

So, how does transitional learning relate to performance improvement? According to Pershing and other HPI academics, transitional learning has been defined as a process of moving from one instance to another. We've already presented the fact that PI is a continuous learning process, where you're working through the different transitions. As previously indicated, there can be issues that affect us during these different transitions, which can affect our performance and output within any situation. Let's put it in the context of a sports team. I am a die-hard Mets and Jets fan, as I am originally from New York. Now, at the age of forty-two, there is not much that I've been able to be happy about in regard to these teams in my life span, but as many New Yorkers know, you're either a Mets-Jets fan or Yankees-Giants fan. What do these teams look to do every year? They want to go to the World Series or the Super Bowl and win the championship, right? How do they attempt to do that? They try to pull from different places to put the best team together. Now, this can be from free agents, from other teams, from the minor league, or from the draft; there are all these different directions that they can take to put a team together that will help them get to the championship game and win. This is exactly what the TLP does. It takes concepts, theories, and models associated with HPI and systems thinking and creates a process, or team in this analogy, which will help us get to the end goal of being successful, or in this case, the championship.

In regards to HPI there are two main models and theories that have been utilized to develop the TLP, and those are the cognitive approach and the strategic planning approach. These two approaches, when combined with the systems thinking idea, is how the TLP was developed and created. The cognitive approach to learning looks at how we understand, how we create and use information. It's concerned with how information is processed by the learner. It focuses on the understanding of information and its concepts. According to Pershing's *Handbook*, previously mentioned, the cognitive approach selects the information, links it with existing information, and organizes and assimilates the information.[2] In short, it helps to build learning skills so we can learn more effectively and efficiently and be successful. In combination, the purpose of the strategic planning approach is to maintain a favorable balance in order to shape and guide our lives. It provides a systematic process for gathering information for specific goals and objectives in the actions that we are trying to accomplish. An individual strategic plan will help us explain how we intend to allocate our resources in order to optimize our objectives and accomplish our goals. The strategic planning approach focuses on the design, analysis, development, and production of performance interventions, and helps us work through the different transitions that we encounter in our life, in our complex system.

In the military, we have what's called the Military Decision Making Process (MDMP) process. This is a form of strategic planning for how we go through different the transitions of the planning process for mil-

---

[2] Pershing, "Designing Instructional Strategies: A Cognitive Perspective," #16.

itary operations. It's focused on military operations and institutes different military techniques, tactics, and procedures. These may be procedures that are present within a military context, but the process is still the same, as it follows the continuous learning idea that we discussed earlier in the chapter. I am sure my fellow service members are familiar with a "Rock Drill." If not, it is a rehearsal so to speak, where we work through and war game possible scenarios of the course of action selected.

Instructional planning, which is the basic framework for developing curriculum, is an example of how strategic planning can be implemented in the workplace or in an academic setting. To support the ideas surrounding these PI approaches, a specified systematic instructional design framework can be used to identify problems and examine specific goals in conjunction with the curriculum you develop for a course of instruction, similar to a Rock Drill. Instructional planning addresses problems and concerns—and barriers or obstacles—while planning for specific goals, achievements, and chosen courses of action. This mirrors the ideas surrounding the TLP.

A systematic approach considers the larger environment, including the pressures, expectations, constraints, and consequences we deal with in our complex system. HPI specifically considers the system as a whole—uncovering problems and issues and looking for the root causes associated with the concern. This is how the proper solution, or a solution within the transition, will address the system as a whole when it's developed. All of the approaches that have been presented in this chapter up to this point present prior knowledge of transitional learning's effective approaches to learning and to innovative ideas for improving performance.

The TLP's Eight Strategies and formula for success were created and developed from the theories and techniques described in this chapter. The next chapter will go into more detail on the TLP, how transitional learning can help, its creation, and how we can get to the next levels in our lives, i.e., in our complex system, when we apply the strategies for success to our everyday lives. I promise that this book will provide you with an in-depth understanding of transitional learning and the TLP strategies, the different aspects of life in our complex system where we may find it beneficial to apply the TLP, and examples of successful ways to implement the Eight Strategies for Success during different transitions in a process. There will be examples of humor, regret, disappointment, and at times sadness, pulling on your heartstrings, but in the end, you will see how beneficial applying these different strategies for success can be to your complex system of life, which truly has no playbook.

To end this chapter, let's look at my decision to write this book. When I completed my doctoral degree in education, I transitioned from graduating college to continuing to working in my given profession. I was excited about my educational accomplishment, which spanned about twenty years in the making. To some that may seem like a long time, but in that time, I learned so much about myself and my own complex system that has brought me to this point. It has helped me to see how passionate I am about education, specifically transitional learning, and how I have transitioned in my own life. I gave myself a timeline of the age of forty to attain my doctoral degree (took me to forty-one years of age, but who's counting) and accomplish my goal. I did achieve my attainable goal by working through the different transitions within my complex system and the barriers and obstacles that followed. As I approached a new transition of figuring out what to do with all this information that I had gathered through my studies, it wasn't even a question—I wanted to write a book.

I am an avid reader. I even read a book to help me read faster so that I could read more books. I'm not going to say that I am not still the butt of the joke from my friends about becoming a speed reader, but it has truly helped me gain more knowledge in life about how we learn, how we understand and comprehend, and how utilizing concepts associated with transitional learning can be beneficial. My attainable goal is to provide you with this information, to help you see how transitional learning and the TLP, with its Eight Strategies for Success, can help you get to these attainable goals in your life. I hope that the content in the remainder of this book will bring you as much success as it has brought me when applied to any obstacle or barrier you face.

The Eight Strategies for Success are sequential, building on one another, and when applied in order, they lay out a systematic process for success. Here is a list of the Eight Strategies for Success:

1. *Presenting New Knowledge*
2. *Presenting Examples*
3. *Integrating Visual Aids*
4. *Practicing and/or On-the-Job Training*
5. *Instituting Feedback and Collaboration*
6. *Administering Tests and Evaluation*
7. *Applying Problem-Solving Techniques*
8. *Utilizing Performance Support Systems*

The Eight Strategies for Success are the framework for the TLP and the premise behind success within transitional learning. To this point, I have provided you with all of the background surrounding PI, systems thinking, and transitional learning that make up the transitional learning process. In addition, I hope the examples and experiences have helped you see how and where transitional learning is present, how it can be applied, and how the TLP can help you succeed and push through your complex system with success. The following chapters are meant to show you how each strategy, when applied in the right way, can help you push through the numerous transitions of life, push through the barriers and obstacles, and live up to your potential and succeed. Trust the process and let's dive in together!

CHAPTER THREE

Trust the Process

Transitions are a part of life. They occur in everything we do and every process we engage with—and they can either produce positive or negative results. The question is not will a transition occur, but how we will react to that transition? Simply, how will we respond? This is where the TLP comes into play. In the previous chapter, I provided a solid background of what influenced the creation of the TLP, but I have not gone into detail about how it can be applied. This chapter focuses on the process itself and how the TLP can help guide you through life's transitions. Trust the process, and it will help you succeed!

I have gone through many memorable transitions in my life; some have shaped my life more than others. My decision to enter the military was at a transition point in my life when I knew a change needed to be made, but I was not 100 percent sure of what was the right decision. I joined the military in 2000, which (as we all know) was before the tragic and unforgettable 9/11 terrorist attacks. This was an occurrence that we will never forget, and a time that every American will always remember. As a true New Yorker, born and raised in Queens and Staten Island, the attacks truly hit home for me. I will never forget where I was when I heard and still have a hard time thinking about it. Like I said, I had joined the military prior to 9/11 and was stationed in Germany with my TACP unit in 2001. As a certified Joint Terminal Attack Controller (JTAC) you are a certified controller in charge of calling in Airstrikes when required. This is a certification within the TACP career field; it takes about three years to attain. It is a lot of responsibility to put on someone, but a job that I loved and am thankful for choosing. On September 11, 2001, I was not a JTAC yet and was in the field training, which means I was supporting a training exercise for the Army. We were called back to the main base and informed of the news. Immediately, I thought of my family and wanted to make sure everyone was OK. The base was on lockdown, and it took me three days to get my dad on the phone because the lines were all jammed up in New York. Fortunately, everyone in my family was OK. My stepbrother had a meeting scheduled in One World Trade Center that morning at 8:30 a.m. but called in sick because he got too drunk the night before. Crazy, right? A crazy night of drinking may have saved his life.

The next year and a half was pretty crazy for me, as we received weekly briefings about what was happening and next steps. I received word I would be heading to Kuwait at the end of 2002 and would be part of the team that invaded Iraq on March 20, 2003. I was still a Senior Airman, E-4, and not a certified controller, so mainly I would assist with maintaining radios and equipment and assist the senior controllers with whatever they needed. It was an exciting time, which I will never forget. I was serving my country in a way that I would have never expected. I was part of a time in history that will be explained to my children in textbooks someday. One thing that you probably won't see in a textbook is a description of the guys on the team I was a part of, driving into Iraq in HUMVEEs, blasting "The Final Countdown" on the radio on "D" day. Fists pumping in the air, screaming and shouting, ready for whatever was coming. For the next few days we transitioned through Iraq, eventually ending up at Baghdad International Airport (BIAP).

The things that I experienced and the things I saw and witnessed are permanently embedded in my brain and will die with me when I leave this earth. I will never forget them. As a twenty-three-year-old young man from Staten Island, New York, the occurrences I witnessed and was a part of is something that no twenty-three-year-old should ever have to see. I give so much credit to the men and women in uniform, who choose to serve this great nation and to the members of coalition forces who work with them every day. So, thank you all. Let me put how surreal it was in context. One night we were all sitting in the building we had stopped at for the night and were watching CNN on a TV the communications unit had set up. We were watching a live report of the fighting in Baghdad on the television, but when you looked out the window, you could see the exact same fighting going on. It truly was surreal.

I spent my twenty-fourth birthday in Iraq—on a flight line awaiting a helicopter flight to a different area of the country. Did I mention there were about three sandstorms that night? But who's counting? I'll be honest, I really can't remember how many, as the entire deployment was surreal, filled with moments that made a distinct impact on my life. My final destination in the country was at BIAP, and there was no shortage of Saddam photos, secret rooms and a bona fide torture bed in one of the offices. I mean it; I got a great photo of it. The experience was truly surreal. I was working through so many transitions at once, I couldn't keep track. I will also say, during that initial deployment, I made some pretty memorable connections with guys I call brothers.

We were all experiencing things that none of us thought we would in our lifetime, during an uncertain time. It was a process to say the least. We all dealt with our transitions in different ways, but we always tried to maintain a sense of humor for each other. One night, we were working in the operations center together on night shift, and one of the guys decided he was going to see how many Meals Ready to Eat (MRE) he could eat in a shift. Dude, those things have like three thousand calories in them. Needless to say, he polished off the better of five to six MREs throughout the night. We laughed more and more with each bite. I am sure he didn't shit for like a week. It was hilarious and memorable. It was how we coped. There are many stories like this—the guy who hugged former Secretary of State Donald Rumsfeld when he shook our hands, the juice box in the eye, the singing, and dead arms. Too many stories to list. It helped.

Now, this is a specific reaction to my experience, and I am sure it was different for everyone involved. The reason I bring all of this up is because I wanted to paint a picture of what I was experiencing, so you could put yourself in my shoes. It is meant to help you see and understand one of the most memorable transitions I have ever faced in my life, which was the transition back into everyday life from Iraq. I had just spent over five months in a place, during a time words cannot describe. Every emotion, question, worry, and excitement you could imagine—at a time and place where every day is a new experience, and it was necessary to elicit just enough fear to make sure you did not get killed. How do you just shut that off? How do you transition? The answer is: however you need to in whatever way works for you. This is where transitional learning plays an integral role—specifically, the ideas and concepts surrounding transitional learning and systems thinking. Trust the process! Look at the complex system of life you are engaged in, and choose the correct path for you, the path that helps you live up to your full potential. Remember, we have a choice. We can deal with our transition and all it entails, or we choose not to deal with it.

Of course, it is not always black and white, and the majority of the time we live in the gray area, but we do have a choice, and the TLP can help us make that choice a successful one as we work through the transition to the best of our ability. My transition process may not look like yours, but it worked for me on this deployment and the three others I have been through. It is not to say I do not deal with the gray area and lingering effects, but I made a choice to keep everything there. I chose to look at it as two different systems of thinking, two different ways of perceiving. First, what happens in the country stays in the country, and second, I will leave it all there. I chose to leave everything in the country, and not bring it home. This helped me see that home was home, and the deployed location is the deployed location. I am a better man for my experiences, but I knew it was not my reality at home. I looked at it as a learning experience, and a process specific to my job and the deployed location. This is how applying the ideas surrounding transitional learning got me through this indescribable experience.

Not everyone agreed with the way I dealt with my transition. I remember shortly after returning home from my first deployment and going back to Staten Island on leave, my father and I went to dinner at a local Italian restaurant we frequented, which was around the block from our house. We sat there, ate good food, had a few drinks, and began discussing what I had gone through. I tried explaining to him how I felt—tried putting into words what my transition was like. The conversation took a turn for the worse when I told him I was not scared over there. My father was a Vietnam veteran, who spent just shy of two years in Vietnam during the war, which I can guarantee was a different experience than what I had just gone through for five months. We actually began arguing a bit about it, as my dad told me that I was scared and it was OK. I, of course, denied it and the argument continued. Was I scared? Did I not want to admit it? Or is it that I just did not see it? Who knows? The one thing I can tell you is that my dad and I both had a different experience with our transitions. We both dealt with it in our own way, but we both dealt with it by learning within our own complex system, as we can learn to trust the process.

I want to share an experience where transitional learning helped me get to the next level in my life. If you have not been able to tell by this point, my father has been a very big part of my life. He is partially responsible for the man I am today, and his influences in my life have been more impactful than words can say. He always knew what I needed, and how to help me, without even trying. He literally saved me when I was sixteen from becoming someone I was not, and brought me back to who I truly am, the irresistible man you see today. Just kidding, of course. He was the greatest person I have ever met, and I know he changed the lives of everyone he encountered. This is why his death was something that I have never truly accepted and never truly gotten over, and it will always leave a void in my life. Today would have been his seventy-second birthday actaully. He is on my mind, and maybe this is why I am telling this story, but it was probably the worst transition I had ever experienced, and I had already been to war. What could I possibly learn from it? I would later find out I learned more than I ever could imagine from this transition.

It was a normal Saturday, just like any other. I was stationed in Fort Riley, Kansas, and had been in the USAF for just over three years at this point. I was living with a friend, sharing a two-bedroom apartment. My roommate had gone to play basketball with some other friends, and I was still recovering from the night before. Just so you can see how close my dad and I were, we used to call him from the bar, and he would get on the phone and talk to girls for us. He was our telephonic wingman and *always* made the girls laugh. He is the guy who could get an entire barber shop pumped by talking about life—just ask my buddy Frank, who sat in a chair waiting while my dad entertained the entire shop. He just made an impact on everyone who knew him. So, I was recovering from Friday night and called my house to speak to my dad. I was going home for Thanksgiving the following Tuesday and wanted to chat with him. We chatted two to three times a week.

My stepmom picked up the phone, and we chatted for a bit. She told me my dad was sleeping still, as he had sleep apnea and would sleep a lot during the day because he did not want to wear his CPAP mask at night. My dad had recently retired after spending over thirty-one years as an electrician in the International Brotherhood of Electrical Workers (IBEW) trade union. My stepmom said she would go wake him up; it was about two thirty in the afternoon. (Yeah, it was a rough Friday night.) My stepmom entered the bedroom, while talking to me on the phone, and out of nowhere I heard her scream. I will never forget what I heard.

"He's blue; he's not breathing! Oh, my God!"

I remember holding my breath and feeling lightheaded. She screamed on the phone, "I'll call you back." I was standing in my apartment, alone, hungover, trying to process what had just happened. The next three minutes felt like an eternity. Every thought, emotion, and feeling went through my body. I could not take it anymore. I called back, and she picked up crying. She continued screaming and crying and again said, "I'll call you back." Now I was getting angry, as the emotions began taking over. All I kept thinking was, "No way." This could not be happening. Finally, I called back again after a few minutes, and my neighbor George picked up the phone. The words that came next are something I will never forget; they were words that changed my life. He said, "Michael, your father is gone."

I hung up the phone and lost it. I had no idea what to do next. I knew I needed to get home, but I also needed to get things in order. Worse, I needed to call my sister and my brother and tell them what happened. I am sure you can imagine how those conversations went. A lot of crying, denial, anger, and so on. My roommate came home, and I was a mess. He hugged me and started crying himself. He took a breath with me, and we began getting things squared away. Within an hour we were on the way to the airport.

The flight home was a blur. I still cannot tell you what went on; I was in a fog. To put it into context, the suitcase I brought home had two pairs of underwear in it with one sock, a pair of jeans, and two shirts. Oh yeah, and my toothbrush. It was a huge suitcase. I arrived at home, and I am sure you can imagine how things were. People in denial, disarray, and beyond the level of sadness. Again, a lot of this was and still is a blur. I felt outside myself. The one person in my life who I could always count on, who helped me and was there for me, was gone. How was I going to do this? How would I transition though my complex system of life without him? I was only twenty-four and needed my dad.

The next day, we went to begin setting arrangements. The funeral director asked if I wanted to see him and I said no. I did not want to remember my dad like that. I wanted to always see the happy, laughing, jolly guy I knew. The wake, funeral, and aftermath came and went. It was a five-day period that will live in my memory forever. I will say that I could not have gotten through it without the love and support of the people in my life. My best friends truly helped me through it and are more brothers to me than friends. Two of them even came from Germany to be there for me. Love you guys; words can't express my gratitude, as I would have fallen apart without you guys. Thanks Frank, Leo, Justin, and Shawn. I am better for knowing you guys.

Now the cause of his death is and will always be a question mark. There was no autopsy done. They said heart attack, but who knows? There were other factors that could have contributed. I am sure you can imagine where I was mentally, emotionally, and spiritually. I was at a transition point. I was at a point when I had to make a decision. Do I choose to give in to my sadness and spiral, or do I push forward and try and heal? At twenty-four years old, I had no idea. So what did I do? I looked at my situation and asked myself, "What would Dad do?" I knew instantly. I needed to use my support system—the people around me—to get through this transition. As you will see later in this book, it is one of the strategies!

I chose to use transitional learning to get me to the next level in my grief and push forward, as I knew my dad would want me to do. I wish I could say I made it through without a hitch. That was not the case at all. His death still haunts me to this day, and it is something I will never fully recover from. I went through many transitions with his death—denial, sadness, loneliness, fear, anxiety; the list goes on. I am forty-one years old, almost twenty years later, and I have just starting accepting it. I have a pretty dynamite therapist who helps me bring a lot of clarity to my life and to the numerous transitions I have gone through. He recommended I write a letter to my dad recently, and I have to tell you, it really helped me lay out my feelings. It's a real tear jerker too, so make sure you get the hankies. I still work through my grief about his death every day; you never truly get over such a traumatic experience without scars, at least in my opinion. It's about getting to the next level, applying what you learned to the process, and moving through the barriers and obstacles.

Remember, we live in a complex system called life. The strategies for success, when applied, will help you live up to your potential and work through these transitions. Remember, we need to trust the process. It needs to be driven by you, as each of us work through different transitions at different points in our life. Remember, we all know what works best for us—how each of us works through our individual learning process. When applied in the proper context, geared toward each person, the TLP and its strategies for success can make all the difference, can change your direction, and can truly change your life if you let it. Trust the process, this is something I cannot say enough; you need to trust yourself within the process to be successful in anything we do. Think about a time in your own life, whenever you hit a roadblock, when you hit a stopping point—a time when a barrier or obstacle was in your way or when you engaged the transition process? Think about that split second when you realized this, when you perceived how something was and what was going to happen or not happen? How did you respond?

I want you to think about this as we go through the Eight Strategies for Success and their components. Each strategy builds on the other, and when combined, they will help you succeed and be better throughout your transitions. Just as the TLP and the strategies for success are sequential, so are the personal experiences provided. I have provided a few to date, but to get a better sense of what the TLP strategies can do, the eight experiences provided will range from childhood through adulthood and even include my current situation. Each experience is from a time in my life when a transition was occurring, and the components of that strategy helped me push through the barrier or obstacle I was facing. The reason I provide examples from childhood through adulthood is to show how the TLP strategies for success can be applied to any transition, at any point in your life. This is a self-help book geared toward adults, but its concepts can be applied at any age. If you take anything from the contents of this book, I hope it's that transitional learning and the TLP strategies can help you succeed. Trust the process and push forward. Let's dive in everyone! You won't regret it.

CHAPTER FOUR

Teachable Moments

Have you ever been presented with new knowledge that you did not know how to process or what to do with it? Have you ever questioned what the next steps were or even what direction you should go? I have. I have had many transitions in my life where I did not know where to go or what to do with the information I was receiving. Fortunately, this is where the first strategy of the TLP process comes into play. Strategy One is titled, *Presenting New Knowledge*. This strategy looks at the barrier or obstacle you may be facing within the transition and views it as new knowledge within your system. It opens your mind to look at the encounter as new knowledge and not necessarily a barrier or obstacle toward success. When applied in this manner, it will expand on your current level of thinking and open the door to new techniques and methods of retaining the information to work for you—not the other way around.

The key is perspective. The ability to view something as a positive encounter, a teaching moment so to speak, and not necessarily a barrier or obstacle—with a negative outcome—is vital to its success. I cannot say this enough: perspective can be something that will make or break you when your back is against the wall. When push comes to shove, we tend to lean into our negative perspectives and give in to the information being received in a way that hurts us instead of helps us. Put yourself in this mindset right now, reflect on this and think about what your default reaction or perspective when new knowledge is provided to you is. It goes back to the cognitive approach to learning and how our mind processes the information. Remember, everything is a process, and we are in charge of our own process within our own complex system of life. Knowledge can be any information received during an experience, so who is to say we have to receive that information in a way that affects our process by hurting our chances for success. The goal is to succeed, so we need to view this new information in a way that helps us—not hurts us.

Think about this: the possibilities for success are endless at this point. I am not saying this will be easy. Some of us see things more cautiously than others, and this is due to our life experiences and prior perceptions. It could be because of things we learned from the influential people in our lives or something that just stuck with us from a personal experience. So, it may take time to change your process, but if you are dedicated to your success, and want to succeed, then they are all learning and teachable moments. Applying this strategy to your process will provide you with new techniques for retaining the information in a way that will assist in your success and not hinder it. It will help you figure out new ways to review, accept, and apply the information to help you succeed. Think about a time within the last twenty-four hours when you received new information, and your perception leaned more towards a negative reaction. This can be anything where you were at a crossroads, and it felt right to lean to the latter. What did you do? Which direction did you go? What outcomes came of it? Most likely, if your perception was negative, then the overall outcome was negative. You were behind the curve from the beginning, so you already jumped the gun at the starting line and faulted. With this analogy in mind, let me tell you about a time in my childhood when I was provided with new information, and my initial perception or reaction to the information was negative. I chose, whether consciously or subconsciously, to see the new information in a negative way.

I told you that the strategies within the TLP are sequential, building on one another, and that when applied correctly, they will help you achieve a successful result. So, it's no surprise that the first example is from my childhood. My family is from New York City, specifically the borough of Queens, New York. My mother is from Astoria and my father grew up in the Woodside projects. They both come from middle class, hard-working families where money was sparse. In New York, the trade unions make up about 20 percent of the construction professions, and my family was no exception to this statistic. My grandparents, uncles, cousins, father, brother—and other family members—all worked in one of the many trade unions. I even spent some time in one of the apprentice programs but quickly realized it was not for me. My parents met in a dry cleaner back in the 1970s. My mother was there picking up dry cleaning, and my dad—well, let's just say the guy working there was his "dealer." My father liked to smoke marijuana back then, and he had stopped in for a dime bag. My father walked my mother home, and that was it. He spent two hours speaking to my grandmother outside, and when he left, my grandmother told my mom she was going to marry that guy. Six months later they were engaged and shortly after they married. I have the pictures of my dad's three-piece white leisure suit. John Travolta would have been proud.

In 1979, they had their second child, me. All three pounds of me. I was two months premature and just over three pounds. I spent six weeks in an incubator in the ICU, and it was touch-and-go at times. I was even named after the doctor who saved my life. My name was supposed to be Scott but that was not in the cards for me, and I was named Michael after the doctor. I will leave his last name out, but he knows who he is, and he is as much to thank for this book as myself. My mother told me I was so small when I came out that they had to dress me in doll clothes. Imagine that. I must have looked like a Cabbage Patch Kid. Being premature did not stop me from pushing forward. I began playing sports from the time I could walk and play. One of the many amazing things my father did for us when we were children was support any choice we wanted to make when it came to extracurricular activities. I grew up in a time before the Internet, cell phones, social media, and the craze within technology we see today. We were outside from dust to dawn, and as many children who grew up in the '80s can attest, we needed to be home when the street lights came on. Yeah, we had Atari and Nintendo (the original NES where you had to blow in the games for them to work), but 90 percent of the time we were outside playing manhunt, sports, or riding bikes. I definitely rode my bike farther than a six-year-old should have by himself—at least, farther than I would let any of my kids ride alone.

I loved to run as a kid. I was OK at basketball, football, and soccer, which means I usually didn't get picked last or anything, but running was definitely my passion—running and swimming. I played football and soccer as well growing up, but I competed in track and field and swimming from about the age of nine through college—and even into the military. Track and field was by far my favorite sport, and although I excelled at the high jump in my later years, running was my forte as a child. I liked the sprint races, specifically the 55-meter dash. As a nine-year-old, I ran track for the county. We had moved from Queens to Massapequa Park, New York, which is on Long Island, when I was four years old. Like I said, I loved to run, so the minute I was able to join the team, I joined. I was pretty good. I began competing and excelled at the 55-meter dash. To a nine-year-old, this was everything. And yes, in case you were wondering, I wore the very flattering singlet and short shorts. (Man, no way could I squeeze in that outfit now, but I bet my wife would like me to try.)

There was one other kid, who ran for a different county, who always gave me competition. I had raced against him one other time, and I had won. I will never forget his name, Aaron, and we were friendly but always gave each other flack during the track meets. So, let's set the mood. It was a windy day but warm. The sun was shining and speed was in the air. I felt super confident and had come in first place the previous two meets. My wall of blue first place ribbons was growing in my bedroom, and I felt like today would be no different. It was a lock! I remember seeing Aaron getting ready with his dad, and my dad and I chatted about it for a second. I remember telling my dad I was going to win, and my dad saying as long as I tried my best, that's all that mattered. My dad was always supportive when it came to sports. He told us kids to try every sport, and we could choose the one(s) we liked, but we were going to do something. This is the same guidance I bring to my boys, and I hope they know I am proud of them no matter what they choose to do! As long as you try your best, you have already won. But as a nine-year--old kid, winning meant being first.

The track felt soft and hot as we lined up. Aaron and I were next to each other, and the tension was high. We knew deep down it was going to be either him or me to cross first. The bullhorn crackled, and I heard "Ready, Set," as I positioned my fingers and raised up like a cat ready to strike: "GO" as the starting pistol went off. If I hadn't been in the zone I may have jumped, but I was dialed in and ready for my next blue ribbon. So, the gun goes off, and we are on our way fifty-five yards to the finish line. I can still put myself in that moment—the air in my face and the feel of Aaron's presence next to me. From what I could see, we were clearly neck-and-neck in the front of the pack. I can see it's close, and I dig deep to push forward. The problem was, Aaron was just as dialed in, and had a step on me. We crossed the finish line first and second, but to my surprise, Aaron had been the better runner that day. He had a good day that day and was the better athlete, something that I did not want to accept at that moment, as the realization of my loss began to set in. This is where the teaching moment came into play.

I remember giving him a quick handshake and congratulations but then turning off to be alone and reflect. This was my transition point, when new information was received. I had lost. I hit a barrier I was not expecting, and I had a choice. I could perceive the information in a negative manner, and react to emotion, or I could take a breath and accept the loss, but see the positive side of it. I came in second. I got to race. The loss would raise my passion to compete and try harder, but most of all, I tried my best. As you can probably guess, I chose the latter, and proceeded to ball my eyes out and get angry. I chose to take the new information of the loss and act out in a negative way.

I proceeded to walk out onto the lawn, sit on the ground, and continue to cry and get angry. My dad approached me and told me to get up. I stood up and turned to him. With loads of compassion, he asked me what was the matter and if I was OK. Now, I know I told you my father was a very understanding guy, but that is not what he said to me at all. It was a long time ago, but I believe it went more like this:

"Why the fuck are you crying?"

I remember being a bit surprised and just looking at him. He put his hand on my shoulder and again asked me why I was crying. He left out the vulgar, colorful expletive this time but again asked me why. I did not have an answer. I looked at him and said, "Because I lost." He now put both hands on my shoulders and looked into my eyes and said simply, "So what." We stood there silent for a second, and he said it again, "So what." This is where the teaching moment sunk in.

He was right. So what! I was so dialed in on perceiving the new information of losing as a negative occurrence that I did not take the time to look at the positive lesson, the perception that helps me see why "so what" is the proper reaction. Now, my father didn't leave it there. He proceeded to give me a hug and tell me I did a great job. He asked me if I tried my hardest, and when I said yes, he told me he was proud of me and that we would work hard to win the next time. He helped me to see that losing the race did not mean anything other than the fact that I lost the race. It didn't change how hard I worked, how good I was, or how much I tried. It simply meant that I lost. When he helped me see that if I perceived the new information in a way that would help me be successful the next time, see ways to succeed and be better, see areas of improvement, and maybe create a new game plan, then I would succeed. Simply put, receiving and reacting to the new information in ways that focused on positive alternatives, instead of focusing on losing or the negative implications of losing, would only assist me in achieving my goals and, in this case, possibly winning the race the next time. Once I did that, the "so what" made all the sense in the world.

I was upset that I lost, but I saw the loss as a teaching moment, a chance to receive the new information and transform it into a positive experience, an experience that would help me succeed. A learning point that could help me be successful and ultimately be better, by applying what I had learned with a positive perspective that would help me achieve the next level of success. That is the overall benefit of the TLP and Strategy One. Receiving the new information and transforming or perceiving it in a positive way—in a way that would assist me in being successful and not hindering my success from the start. In life, if we start from behind, it can take additional time and effort to move forward—compared to if starting from a place of advancement. Take a race like in this example. If we start late, or false start, or don't get a good jump, then we are already starting in the catch-up position, and as I am sure we have all experienced, when we are playing catch-up, it brings additional stress and concern on top of the obstacle or barrier we are already facing with the transition.

Strategy One is the starting point in the process. It could possibly be the most impactful strategy within the TLP, as it sets the tone for the remaining strategies and ultimately the way we observe and reference the transition we are attempting. The most beneficial aspect, at least in my opinion, is that the TLP is a sequential process which builds on itself. You have heard the saying "strength in numbers," right? Well, think about what happens when we apply a step or strategy to an obstacle or barrier. Think about the odds for success when we apply one strategy compared to eight strategies. We probably have a better chance for success with eight then one right. I have applied this type of thinking in my complex system of life, specifically within my military career. Being a member of the military means you are part of a team, especially in the TACP career field where I spent the majority of my career. You are a member of a two-man team, but when shit hits the fan, you need to work together to build on one another to get the job done—whether it be the ground controllers, radio operators, ground troops, or pilots from above. To accomplish the primary goal of bringing everyone home safe and provide air coverage, you need to process and receive the information you have been given in a way that will benefit you and the team.

Starting the process with Strategy One has helped me accomplish many goals I have set in my life and overcome obstacles and barriers I have experienced in my everyday life, education, and career. Strategy One is the starting point in the TLP, since it is when we receive the new information regarding the transition. The TLP assists you with looking at this new information in a positive way; starting from this place will only assist with being successful while applying the remaining seven strategies. Each transition has its own barriers and obstacles and its own form and type of information.

Lets go back to the exercise I mentioned in the beginning of the chapter. I want you to take a minute and reflect on any given twenty-four hour period in your life where you can remember experiencing new information. This could be while you were a student and had a job, or while you were at work and got a phone call from family, or a comparable experience—any time where you were dealing with something and new information came into play requiring you to transition from one point to another with a barrier or obstacle causing additional stress or anxiety during the transition. We have all been there and felt like we were drowning or needed a boost or support. Strategy One provides you with a way to start the transition process on a positive level and in a way that will assist in your success and not hinder it. It institutes a starting point to the TLP, one that begins in a beneficial way and helps you see the transition and its obstacles or barriers in a way so you can say, "So what?" Strategy Two is where we see examples of what to do with the new information.

Once the information is received, Strategy Two, titled *Present Examples*, initiates the next step in the process. This will be discussed in the next chapter, and to follow suit, an example will be given so you can see how utilizing the *Recall and Review* techniques associated with examples will assist in processing the newly received information and achieving success—while overcoming the transition and its associated barriers in front of you. We have noticed and accepted the teachable moment, perceived the new information in a positive way, but now it is time to relate to the information. Now we see how we can utilize examples, the Recall and Relate method to move to the next level in achieving success. Members of the military tend to "learn by fire" on most occasions. Things are not always laid out for you and presented in a way where you can interpret the meaning off the bat. Whether its new techniques, tactics, procedures, equipment, requirements, or some other unfamiliar appraoch, there will most definitely come a point where you will achieve the deer-in-the-headlights look and be lost. Reviewing or recalling other examples of the new information will only increase your knowledge and exposure to the barrier or obstacle within the transition and bring you one step closer to success. One step closer to achieving your goals. Remember, it's a process, and we need to trust the process.

CHAPTER FIVE

Rinse and Repeat

As discussed in the last chapter, anytime we are presented with new information we have a choice to either accept it, and perceive the information in a positive way, or focus on the negative aspects of not understanding the information. Either way, the information is new, and one of the most productive ways to relate to the information is by applying previous examples. This is where Strategy Two comes into play: *Presenting Examples, or Recall and Relate Techniques.* When applied to transitional learning and encountering obstacles or barriers associated with new information, the Recall and Relate technique can assist the individual by applying relatable examples to help process and perceive the information in hopes of achieving a successful outcome. Some benefits associated with Strategy Two are that it provides different avenues for relating to new information, it introduces techniques to help recall the new information through the use of examples, and it can assist in utilizing available templates to apply the new information to your current obstacle or barrier. Most importantly, it initiates the idea of applying previously accomplished work or examples in order to Recall and Relate the content associated with the new information.

Now, I know this may sound a bit confusing, but the Recall and Relate technique is simply a *rinse and repeat* process. We look through our catalog of previously perceived information (examples we may be familiar with) and then apply them in order to help understand the new information. We then repeat, or relate, the concepts associated with the example to our current situation with the hope of being able to interpret and understand the information with a successful outcome. The ultimate goal is to surpass the barrier or obstacle associated with receiving the new information by recalling and relating prior examples to the process within our complex system. The intriguing and exciting part is that you can apply the rinse and repeat technique as many times as you like with as many examples as you need to help process and understand the new information and achieve success in overcoming the barriers and obstacles in our complex system of life.

So, why are examples important? Think about any set of instructions or directions you look at when building something or putting something together. I am not referring to IKEA furniture, as I have still not mastered this maze after forty-one years (but man, they do have some good deals don't they? And where else can you get delicious three-dollar Swedish meatballs as you shop for a couch?). The directions and instructions I am referencing come with examples to help you see what the overall outcome should be. I am a father of two amazing boys, who are currently five and eight years old. They are typical boys who are into cars, trucks, superheroes, sports, and of course—LEGOS! Yes, they both are obsessed with all the different types, colors, sizes, and shapes of Legos. I have spent endless hours (yes, hours) putting together the many different genres of Legos. At times, I have been successful, and at times, my wife has taken over before I destroy the entire thing. I will admit, my fingertips have gone numb on many occasions, especially around Christmastime or birthdays. One thing I will say is Lego instructions have advanced since I was a kid. Now, each step comes with a photo and shows you where you should be in the process and what the lego should look like. Remember, if we break something down into manageable steps within a process, anything is possible. My point is, that when we are provided with an example, it is easy to see the firetruck with the attached hose, or the cop motorcycle with the ATM and bank robber. In all seriousness, when we can relate the information we are struggling with to a relatable example, our chances of success are that much stronger.

Let's put it into perspective. Think about a time when you were provided with new and unfamiliar information. You have already made the conscious choice to perceive the information in a positive way, but now you are trying to relate to the information, so you begin to recall examples you may have encountered in the past where the information was present. You do this (rinse and repeat) technique numerous times, and each time, your overall understanding of the concept begins to increase. This is how Strategy Two fits into the TLP process. Think about the impact this can have on your confidence, your perception, and your ability to overcome the obstacle or barrier in front of you. Remember, it's a process, and if we trust the process, the sky's the limit. You have made a choice, and this choice to reflect on prior examples is ultimately helping you succeed within the process.

We have to remember that all examples may not be positive. This is not a bad thing. As previously discussed, our complex system of life is full of gray areas, times when the outcome is not what we wanted, not where we wanted it to go, and not what we expected. This is a reality, and even more of a reason to remain positive and push forward in the process. Not because we enjoy failing, stumbling, or falling, but because we enjoy getting up, succeeding, and overcoming the odds. Vince Lombardi's quote says it all, "It's not whether you get knocked down, it's whether you get up." That is what matters, how you react to falling. Failure is a part of life, but it's what we do when we fail that makes a difference. My boys are little, but I try to put this into perspective for them. At this stage, it's a missed baseball or incorrect spelling word, but I am trying to get them to understand that if they are engaged with new information that may not feel good, just as I was after the race I lost, what we do next is what makes all the difference. We reflect on these examples, whether good or bad, to help us push forward and succeed. These are all transition points in our process, times when we have to make a choice, and if we continue to look at the encounter in a positive way and attack the process in a way in which we can then succeed, the outcome will be favorable.

Let's look at another example that most of us can relate to as adults. When I exited the military (active duty that is), I was at a transition point in my professional career. My goal was to finish college, but I had to work as well. I started looking at the different platforms available for open jobs (Internet, newspaper, etc.) and began applying. I started going on interviews, and with each interview, I learned more and more of what was needed to do well and hopefully be offered the job. It even became an event among my friends, as we started keeping track of my record of being selected. I had no clue what I wanted to do, so I just kept waiting for the next best thing to come along. The reason I bring this up is because preparing for a job interview is the perfect place to utilize the Recall and Relate technique. Before the interview, speak with people who have interviewed for a similar position, watch videos and examples, and finally, think about interviews you have done. Think about what worked and what didn't work, and apply these ideas to the next one. Rinse and Repeat. One final point on this—a gem or nugget of information that can be helpful when interviewing—make sure to ask at least three questions at the end of the interview. Do your research for the first two, but the final question needs to be something along the lines of, "Is there anything else I can elaborate on in my resume or background—or that we discussed today—that can help me move to the next stage in the hiring process?" Leave nothing on the table!

In keeping with the sequential process of steps that build on one another, the personal experience I want to discuss for this strategy occurred a few years after the lost race. I can remember it like it was yesterday, and it was a pivotal time in my life when I used the Recall and Relate technique of presenting examples to help me push past a barrier or obstacle. I was eleven years old at the time, so we need to remember that and put it into context. The barrier or obstacle was serious to a fifth grader. It was the summer before fifth grade began, and like many other ten to eleven year olds in the 1980-90s, my days consisted of riding bikes, eating Twinkies, playing sports and manhunt, and staying up all night at a sleepover with my friends drinking Jolt Cola (yeah, I actually drank that shit) and playing Contra on Nintendo. Sounds fun, right? Recently, I showed my eight-year-old Super Mario Bros II on an old NES, and he mastered it in hours. Times have definitely changed, my friends. Back to the story, I remember, it was the beginning of August, and I was counting down the days until Labor Day. As kids growing up in New York know, we went back to school on the Tuesday after Labor Day. It was a Saturday morning, and I was enjoying a bowl of Lucky Charms while watching G.I. Joe on TV. The phone rang, and I remember hearing my dad on the phone saying he would be in soon and would take care of the problem.

My dad was an electrician. Most of my family worked in the different trades—Teamsters, pipefitters, plumbers, and such. All I knew to that point was my dad helped put up the lights for the Rockefeller

Center Christmas Tree at Christmastime, which was pretty cool to a kid. I knew he took the bus to work and came home after school ended and before dinner. He worked late and weekends sometimes, but I could always count on hearing his keys and work boots when he opened the door most days. On this Saturday, my mom was shopping with my sister, and my brother was god knows where; he had recently turned fourteen and was living the life of a teenager. So my dad said to me, "Let's go, you're coming with me to work." I was so excited. I loved working with my hands and putting things together as a kid.

I enjoyed working through things with my hands as a kid, creating things. I used to empty the junk drawer at my grandmother's house and build anything I could with what was there. I worked on models, played with Legos and blocks, and used to build anything I could with spare parts and pieces. I didn't have plans, I just enjoyed not knowing what it would be. It was pretty cool imagining things as I wanted and not necessarily what they were. My dad told me I had a good imagination, and my mom said maybe I would be an engineer one day. I had no clue what an engineer was, but it sounded cool. So, my dad and I headed out. At that time, my dad was in the J division of Local 3, which was a local within the IBEW. The J division mainly worked in building maintenance, and my dad was the electrician for the building. The fire alarm system had an electrical failure, and the system would not turn off. They called my dad in to fix the system, as the fire department had already been notified, but they could not turn it off. I remember thinking how cool it all was and watching my dad work with his tools just enhanced my excitement.

My dad finished the work, and he and the building engineer were standing in front of the main system box. This was controlled by a computer that ran the system. My dad called me over and told me what was going on. He explained things to me in a way that an eleven-year-old would understand, and then asked me if I wanted to put the final touches on fixing the system. I was ecstatic and jumped at the opportunity. As an adult, I can see all I did was push a button, but as an eleven-year-old kid, I thought I fixed it all. My dad explained to me that building engineers designed the system—that they created how the system worked and how it could be fixed—but people like my dad actually worked on fixing and maintaining them. He said, "They build the instructions for it, you know, like you like to do." I thought that was so cool!!! I felt like, now, I understood what an engineer did, and I wanted to be one so bad.

The summer ended and fifth grade started. My obsession with becoming an engineer heightened. I began finding out more and more about what engineers did and that there were all different kinds of engineers. I found out that engineers used math and made good money, but most importantly, that engineers created and built stuff. They created the directions and the instructions that went along with what they built! At least, this was my interpretation of what an engineer was at eleven years old. We all know there is more to being an engineer than just this; it is an amazing field with so many directions and opportunities to explore. For this story, however, this is what an engineer was to me. So, when my fifth grade project—a class project where each student would write about what they wanted to be when they grew up—approached, I felt confident in my ability to do well.

We created a mural for the class wall, and each student drew themselves as an adult working in their chosen field. Each student had to write a report as well, outlining their profession, what they knew about it, and how they could accomplish their goal. I remember being upset about my initial drawing but after making numerous attempts at it, I was very happy with the final result. I will never forget it. I had a hard hat, shirt, tie, slacks and dress shoes—a wrench in one hand and blueprints in the other— and was standing in front of a computer fire alarm system. Yes, I wanted to be a building engineer, creating the blueprints and ideas surrounding the different systems that controlled the building. The inner workings of a building really interested me and so did the engineer who helped bring it to life.

I sat down to write my report and hit a wall. I spent so much time focusing on the mural picture that I forgot about the report aspect of the project. I remember feeling overwhelmed, scared, nervous, and angry. My father came home from work, keys jingling and boots loudly stomping across the floor. He came into the dining room where I was sitting at the table. I guess he could see the worry on my face because he asked me what was wrong. I explained everything to him, and told him I did not know what to do. I did not know how to write down what I was thinking and how to phrase everything like I drew in the picture. I was at a transition point, an obstacle or barrier that hindered me from finishing my report. My father smiled at me and said, "Write about what you know, son." He began talking to me about that day when I came to work with him. He had me thinking about what I had seen, experienced, and done. We talked about the conversation we had on the way home and all of the things we discussed and looked at between that day and today regarding being an engineer.

As my dad continued to speak, I could feel the anxiety lessen and lessen inside of me, as I began thinking about examples of the many things I had reviewed and looked at about engineering. It all started from that one example of when I went to work with him, but it continued to build and build as I recalled and related information, reviewed examples, and applied them to the obstacle, which was completing the report. I took the new information and looked at it in a positive way, then recalled examples and related them to what I knew, understood, and experienced in relation to the project. I did this many times with my dad, until I felt as confident as I did in the beginning of the project. Remember, it's a process, and if we trust the process, we can overcome any obstacle. The beauty of the TLP is that you can work through the process and it's Eight Strategies as many times as you need. If you get through the strategies and need to reattack one for clarification and guidance, the process is set up to help you be successful. In this case, I started the process in a confident state, feeling positive about Strategies One and Two; but I took a step back during Strategy Two. I needed to reset Strategy One and then continue into Strategy Two with the same mindset. Rinsing and repeating in a positive way helped me to be successful in the end. Rinse and repeat. This is a term we use a lot in the military, since training is a large part of preparing for combat. So, I am no stranger to working through obstacles numerous times before feeling confident in the final product and ultimately being successful.

I remember sitting with my dad, going over the information, feeling great about the direction I was taking with the project. My dad sat with me a little, but once he could see I was on a role, he left me to my imagination. I felt alive writing the report, recalling and relating the experiences and examples I wrote down as if I were there again. I could see them clear as day, and the words flew out on the paper—similar to now, writing this book. I know it may be hard to believe, but I didn't decide to write this book this morning with no reflection or research. This book is forty-one years in the making, but the concepts behind the TLP have been reviewed and recalled and related to over the last six years while completing my doctorate degree in education. As I stated in the beginning of the chapter, the concepts may appear in-depth at times, but the premise behind the strategy is simple, and my hope is that the personal experiences and examples provided only enhance your understanding and give you the chance to Recall and Relate to the information in your own way. This is a process, and if we trust the process, we can be successful.

The TLP is all about transitional learning and working through the different obstacles and barriers at the numerous transition points in our complex system of life. I cannot say it enough, if we break life down into manageable steps within the process, then anything is possible. The concepts associated with systems thinking mirror this idea; everything in life is a process. Life is a complex system with many processes and transition points, and it is up to us how we want to approach these challenges.

Let's go back to the fifth grade project: the mural and report. There were many steps within the process, and as each transition approached, I chose the direction I wanted to take. These choices weren't black and white—some were positive and others were negative—but in the end, I trusted the process and my ability to work through the process. I was successful. My dad reviewed my report and told me he was proud of the job I did, and when I submitted it, my teacher returned it with positive feedback and comments. She said she was pleased with the detail and that it seemed like I knew a lot about being an engineer.

My eight-year-old son loves trucks, cars, and trains. He is always drawing, building, and creating new types of automobiles and transportation vehicles. I have had many conversations with him about becoming an engineer but have never told him that's what he has to do. I make sure he knows that Daddy will always be proud of him, no matter what he chooses to be, as long as he tries his best! We look at engineering books for kids and talk about creating things—I even bought him graph paper because he likes to draw "constructions," (he means instructions). I don't "make" him do anything; I guide and support him and make sure he knows he can be anything he wants as long as he works hard. Both of my sons are sharp, smart boys, but they need help just like anyone else. I try to be there for them in the same way my father was for me. Parenting is also a process, one with no "contructions."

The same relationship exists in the workplace between the supervisor and the subordinate. It's about guiding, coaching, and mentoring. We should never tell people what to do but show them how to do it and help them do it themselves. A good leader is only as good as their team, and a strong team is formed by providing the right examples and helping team members relate to what works—but ultimately—making sure they are confident, capable, and successful at completing their work and required tasks (an outcome we strive for from childhood through adulthood). I never became an engineer, as my life took a different direction, but I regret nothing. I followed my passion and calling, just as I will tell my boys to do in their life. My eight-year-old wants to be an engineer today, and my five-year-old wants to "be a worker," as he explains. This will probably change many times in the next ten years, but one thing will remain the same: that Daddy is always here to support anything they want to do and will always be here to help them succeed as long as they try their best and work hard. It's all a process, and if we trust the process we can be successful.

My sons are visual learners, like many kids their age. They like to see visual examples, or visual aids, of the different things they are interested in. We color and draw all the time, and my sons want me to help them draw different figures, objects, and so forth. Well, they don't normally ask for help, it's more like, "Daddy, can you draw me this or build me that." Sometimes I give in, but most times I help and guide them to do it themselves. They learn by seeing and by visualizing what they need to do but also by seeing how success is possible, just like their dad. I am sure many of you can relate to this idea of learning by seeing. Visual aids and illustrations are often incorporated into on-the-job training, seminars, workshops, etc. The integration of visual aids is a strategy that supports visual learners, and it just so happens to be the third strategy in the TLP. So let's visualize the next chapter in this book together

CHAPTER SIX

It's Human Nature

As we move through our complex system of life and transition from one experience to the next, one of the primary ways we perceive information is through sight. It's human nature to look at something in an attempt to perceive it in a way that we find relatable. In the first two strategies, we receive the new information and then recall and relate the information to something from our memory. Our ability to now visualize the information in a positive and productive way is imperative to achieving success. As you will see with all of the strategies, a positive mindset—the framework behind the process—is needed for a successful outcome. The way we perceive something may not be the same as the way others view it, so it is important to use the knowledge, know-how, and other techniques we are familiar with while both receiving and dispensing new information.

Strategy Three focuses on the integration of visual aids to assist in receiving, recalling, and dispensing the new information in order to overcome the obstacles or barriers we face within the transition. Remember, we are applying this strategy to new information we are struggling with during a transition point in our complex system of life. It is human nature to visualize things in a way that helps us understand the new information. Integrating visual aids will assist in transforming the information through illustrations and/or text layout. Methods associated with Strategy Three will look to apply the new knowledge and information to visual aids for more in-depth interpretation, implementing the new ideas and innovative techniques through illustration—maybe utilizing social media and technology to initiate an understanding of the new information, creating different training tools (such as worksheets, handouts, or slide presentations) and developing learner-centric tools such as hands-on exercises and activities (my favorite). These are just some of the examples driven by Strategy Three, with the overall goal of transforming the new information through illustrations and/or text—simply put, the integration of visual aids within the transition process.

As we discussed in the beginning of the chapter, it is human nature to perceive what we see in relation to our experiences, so why not integrate visual aids in our TLP to achieve success and push through the barriers and obstacles we face within the transition. It is just another positive tool for success within the numerous transitions we encounter in our complex system of life. Life is full of transitions, and within those transitions, we are sure to encounter new information that we may struggle with. Visualizing success through the use of illustration and/or text, will only help with achieving your goal of success. Visual aids can be anything from pictures, books, presentations, props, tools, and so on—any form of illustration that helps the individual visualize the information in a positive way. This practice has helped many people perceive and dispense new information in a way that they can relate to—a way that assists them in pushing past a barrier and ultimately being successful during the many transitions in their lives.

We all face trying times or times when we are scared and nervous, second-guessing our abilities. Strategies One and Two help to receive and relate the new information, whereas Strategy Three helps to illustrate it. For some, including myself, we learn better by seeing or doing, so the integration of visual aids is a very useful tool in the TLP. Whether the visual aid is used to trigger a memory, illustrate a thought, or just assist in moving through the transition, it can be extremely beneficial to the transition process when applied in a positive way. Remember, it is all a process and we need to trust the process and our own abilities in order to be successful. Optimism versus pessimism—that is the key to success. I love the saying, "We need to see the glass half full instead of half empty." It demonstrates the positive idea which surrounds the TLP and its strategies for success. If we visualize a positive response, and continue on this path, then the outcome will be positive in nature. The cognitive ideas within the TLP focus on how we learn and how our mind interprets the things we see, placing them within our own complex system of life. It's like a Filofax or Rolodex. As we move through life, our perceptions change depending on the situation and the new information received. It is human nature to relate the information to something familiar. When we want to find something, or relate to it, we look through the many files within our brain and bring it to the surface for use. Visual aids can assist with this form of recollection, as things stand out in our mind when they are visualized.

As already noted, I love to read. I even read a speed-reading book—*10 Days to Faster Reading* by Abby Marks-Beale—that helped me read faster and with greater comprehension. My interpretation of the book was not to assist with learning how to comprehend everything but to provide readers with techniques to comprehend the main points and concepts behind the reading in a quicker and more comprehensive fashion. This method helps readers remember the important aspects by skimming and visualizing, breaking the sentences into three parts, and pulling out key words that help to recognize the main ideas surrounding the reading. As I worked through the different exercises in the book, my comprehension percentage and word count increased. Ultimately, I went from reading one hundred and fifty words a minute to around nine hundred words a minute. I have set a goal to read one book a week on a variety of subjects, and I am happy to say, I am sticking to my goal. The reason I bring this up is because the speed-reading book was an example of a visual aid: it was a text layout illustration that helped me push through the transition to reading faster (overcoming the obstacle of reading too slowly) and with added comprehension. This idea truly works when applied to the numerous transition points in our complex system of life.

Reflect on a time in your life when you approached a difficult transition—it can be anything from riding a bike to your first job interview. Think about how you prepared to attack the transition and how you visualized success through the transition (we all play the *what if* game in our minds). Did you utilize any visual aids in this process? Now remember, this does not have to be a picture or illustration but can be any tangible aid you can see and apply to the transition. Did it help? Did it help you see that success was possible? What was the outcome?

We are fortunate in our lives to see success occur at many turns and points. This is something I tell my boys all the time and something my dad told me on a consistent basis. There are so many examples of people who defied the odds, who worked hard towards achieving a goal, who failed, who lost, who stumbled—but always got up and persevered towards success. They visualized success—and probably used some form of visual aid to assist in the process and push through the transition point. Sometimes it is a struggle, and the barrier seems impossible to push past, but remember, if we break it down into manageable steps, anything is possible, including success. This is something I had a tough time seeing as a child, as my self-esteem wasn't always at the climactic point it is now. Of course, I am being facetious and humorous here. We all struggle with insecurity at times, but as a child, I struggled with feeling unwanted, or important, and it hit a tipping point when my parents decided to divorce.

I had a very good childhood in my opinion; I truly cannot complain, as I had two parents who loved me and took very good care of me. I know a lot of so-called self-help books talk about tragic times as a child, and I have all the sympathy in the world for their situation. But, this book is meant to inspire, to make you think, to make you laugh, and at times, to make you see that we all encounter struggles, and it may not be as vivid or obvious as others. I was what they called a latchkey kid. Both my parents worked and my brother, my sister, and I were often alone after school. Of course, until we were a certain age my parents had people watch us, but once my brother turned thirteen or fourteen, we were instructed to head home right after school and do our homework before we went outside to play. I grew up in a middle-class household. It did not appear that we struggled nor were we swimming in dough. We had food on the table, took small family trips, and had presents at Christmas and our birthdays. To a child, this was more than enough.

My mom worked in a bunch of different jobs when I was a child. She was a nurse, worked for the airlines, hotels, and other high-level administrative positions. One thing I can say about my mom is that no matter what job she went for, she always achieved success at a high level. My dad was very different. My dad was a blue-collar worker whose main interest was not the size of his paycheck but that it provided for his family and ensured he was home in time to take us to Marjorie Post Pool (my brother and sister remember those nights) over summer vacation. He was an electrician in the union, worked for Johnson Controls, and made a good living, but we all knew we weren't financially wealthy. My mom had a different outlook on money—and as this is not in any way a dig at her or her morals—but having a lot of money was more important to her than it was to my dad. I used to hear family members say my mom had champagne taste on a beer budget. As a kid, you do not see these things, but I can see now, and she has even admitted to me that she lived well above her means, that it put a strain on their marriage and our family life.

I remember my parents fighting, as most do, but they both did a great job of hiding the issues from the kids, and keeping us out of it. Like I said, I had a very happy, fulfilling childhood—at least until I was twelve years old. That is when my entire world ended (as I knew it), and my parents told us they were getting divorced. This was the early '90s, and things were different back then. Divorce was not what it was in the '50s and '60s, but it still wasn't as accepted and prevalent as it is today. I remember, when they told us they were getting divorced, I remember being the only kid in my grade whose parents were divorced. I have two very distinct memories from that time, which I will never forget. First, I remember going with my dad to Nobody Beats the Wiz, which was a music store in New York back then. He bought a CD, yes a CD, to play for my mom. That was his move, music. He could dance with the best of them and sing like an angel. Well, at least he thought he could sing. I remember sitting on the couch with them while my dad sang "Always Forever" to my mom, trying to hold her hand and see if there was any way to salvage the marriage. I remember my mom's face clear as day. She did not seem very interested at all. I could see in her eyes that the marriage was over. Personally, I think my mom thought the grass was greener on the other side, but as I have discussed with my mom later in life, it's not always greener. The unknown is just that—unknown, and before making choices, we need to really evaluate our current situations. Theres good in everything and everyone, at least that's my opinion.

The second memory was where my transition of their divorce truly took a blow. I am one of three children, the middle child. We all know what it means to be the middle child. My brother is the oldest and my sister is the youngest. They both needed more help with school than I did, since they both suffered from dyslexia. As the middle child, I usually felt left out. It was nothing any of them were doing, just the middle child syndrome we all hear about. It didn't help, though, when my brother used to tell me I was adopted because I had blonde hair as a child, and we come from Spanish and Italian descent, primarily. Now, of course, this was a joke, and typical sibling bullshit. My brother, my sister, and I still talk about the good times as kids, as we were close and have lots of great memories. For some reason, my sister remembers most of them, or she is making them up—something my brother and I are convinced of sometimes (just kidding, Karachi Malachi). All I have to say about that is "Suicide Blonde," boogie boarding with Jay, and I am a Unicorn. You guys know what that's about (love you guys very much).

My sister was the only girl, and Mommy's little girl, and my brother was the oldest—a bit of a problem child, so my dad needed to pull his weight at times. I was usually left in the middle, and it really affected me and my levels of insecurity as a child. This was no different when they divorced, as my sister was going with my mom and my brother with my dad. My parents said to me, verbatim, "You choose where you want to go, Michael." Can you even imagine what that does to a twelve-year-old kid whose parents are divorcing? Not only was my life completely changing, but then I had to choose where I wanted to go. My dad made it clear that it was my choice, and my mom tried to let me decide also—but I knew she wanted me to go with her. I was at a transition point, and I did not know what to do. So, I made the only logical choice I could at that age—I went with what I knew. My mom was moving out of the town we lived in, and my dad was staying there. So, I stayed with my dad. I figured I would feel better being around what I knew, and honestly, I felt safer with my dad's situation. My mom was moving somewhere I did not know with someone I barely knew, so it only made sense to stay where I felt safe. Oh, did I mention I started middle school, which meant I was going to a new school with new kids? There was a lot going on for this twelve-year-old kid.

After the dust settled, and my mom moved away, my dad, my brother, and I moved into a two-bedroom apartment. My parents sold the house we lived in and went their separate ways (at least as much as they could with three kids together). I am sure my dad was struggling, because I knew how I felt, and it was not good. My brother acted out and continued to spiral, hanging with a bad crowd, so my dad did what he could to help himself and us boys. For himself, he started exercising. Dude killed it! Dropped down to 180 pounds, got an earring, and tried growing a ponytail. Hey, it helped so don't judge. He enrolled my brother in karate to help with his temper, and for me—well, nothing. Remember, I was always "OK," right? He did try and help us; he brought us to counseling as a family, the three of us. The counselor looked like The Fonz, but we will keep his name out of it. He was nice and tried to help. We went once a week at 7:00 pm for a few months, and that was where my transition of the divorce took a turn for the better.

I was struggling. I was processing the new information and trying to see the positive. I was trying to relate it to anything I could. Crazy what you think about as a kid. I remember an episode of Family Matters where they talked about divorce, which I thought about a lot. I especially loved movies and television shows as a kid. That was my way of recalling and relating new information. Honestly, it's scary how much I remember from movies, and if you ask my wife, she'll say, "Of course you know that guy's name."

All and all, nothing seemed to help. I was very sad and depressed and could not figure out how to change direction—how to transition off this path. One session, the counselor asked me what I was thinking and if there was anything I wanted to say. I decided to voice my feelings, no matter how scared I was. I told my dad how alone I felt in this and how hurt I was because I felt he cared more about my brother than me. How come I couldn't take karate? How come he didn't do anything for me? Well, at the time, it seemed to go over well, but the next morning my dad bit my head off because of it and said it wasn't fair for me to say that. I was crushed, I felt more alone than ever now. Looking back on it now, and being a father myself, I know my dad was scared; he didn't know what to do and did not react the right way. Remember, we are all human and make mistakes, and he was no different. During the next session with the counselor, I felt even worse than ever. He must have sensed it because he seemed to know something was wrong. The counselor could see that I had a big imagination, that I was creative, and that I liked to write stories. During the next session, the counselor recommended that I keep a journal and write down my feelings.

I've mentioned in previous chapters that I liked to build stuff as a kid, but I also liked to write. My mom was a very good student, very smart, especially in English. She loved to read and write, so I am sure my passion for books and writing came from her influence. I wrote a book when I was in elementary school called, *Johnny Crow, the Dynamic Detective*, and a play titled, "The Christmas Disaster," which my sister and I performed. We made all the props and costumes and even had an intermission with snacks and beverages. We liked to put on shows for our family, and it is a memory that will always live with me. The book and play were pretty good from what I was told. I also attempted to write a song, which was not so good. The words were as bad as my voice—I tried to sing it and fake play the guitar. "Families Forever" will never make it to the Billboard top one hundred list; I pretty much can guarantee that.

But I thought a journal was a great idea and was excited to get cracking. I remember the book I had too. It was a book I found at the drug store; it had a blue hardback cover. I started the journal by discussing how I felt. For three days I wrote in it nonstop about my feelings. The words just flew out of my blue Bic pen onto the paper. I got emotional at times; I cried and felt sad. As time continued over the three days, though, I surprisingly began to feel a huge weight lifted off my chest. After the three days, I started reading everything I wrote. I had written about twenty pages in the journal, so it took me a few days to review and reflect on the information. I noticed how hurt I truly was—not just about the divorce but about the other aspects associated with the divorce. I realized my self-esteem issues heightened because of the divorce, as it made me feel even more alone and unwanted. Specifically, I noticed the damage instilled in me by having to make "the choice," which we referenced later in therapy sessions as an adult.

I really thought about this—how hurt I was that my parents put that kind of pressure on me at a point when I needed help, guidance, and most importantly, love. I am not sure of many things in life, but one thing I am sure of is that love is not a word, it's an action. You can tell someone you love them a million times, but it is the one time you make them feel love that it truly makes a difference. This is where my hurt came from. I did not feel the love and support I needed from my parents at a time when I needed it the most. I felt abandoned, alone, scared, and defeated.

I needed my parents, and they left me out to dry. I needed to feel loved.

The next two weeks were very important to my transition. I wrote and wrote in my blue journal. I continued to write negative feelings, and something that I was not expecting happened: positive feelings began to surface. As I reflected on my hurt, I was also able to see things from my parent's point of view and the things they may have been feeling. I was happy for my dad, as I could see him feeling happy at times as he moved forward and not backwards. It was something that I truly don't think I would have been able to see if I didn't integrate the visual aid of text (in the form of a journal) into my transition process.

It helped me Recall and Relate the new information and transform it into positive thoughts. It helped me make a needed transition. It helped me succeed. We stopped going to see the counselor after about six months, but I will never forget what he did for me, and I continued to use the visual aid of writing in my future transitions, especially when it came to my dad. When my dad passed away (a transition point we already touched upon), my stepmom gave me a few boxes with his stuff in it. As I went through the boxes, I found things that I didn't know he kept. Cards, clothes, pictures, and, of course, many of the "feelings letters" I wrote to him to describe my issues through a transition point. He kept them, and it just showed me how much they meant to him—just as much as they meant to me.

I wish I could say things got easier for me with my parents, but they didn't. I was able to work through my transition of the divorce by using Strategy Three, but the issues between them continued, mainly from my mother. She did not make it easy for us, and after about a year, she convinced me to move in with her, my sister, and my stepdad. The next three years were not very good, as issues continued between my parents—and between my mom and stepdad. I was in the center of a dysfunctional household with my mother and stepdad fighting and arguing. I was not feeling very loved. It was hard and it changed me—adding to my insecurity. It truly damaged my confidence. Don't get me wrong, there were still some good times, and my sister and I got very close during this time. Ultimately, it was not where I was supposed to be or meant to be.

Fortunately, at the end of my sophomore year, my dad came to see me after work one day and told me he did not like the person I was becoming. I was not myself, and I seemed sad, depressed, and scared—not who I am at all. He was right. I broke down and cried to him in a way I hadn't cried in years, and it was like a fountain just pouring out emotions. He hugged me and told me he wanted me to come live with him. I remember feeling so happy and so relieved, as if I could take off this wrinkled suit I had on and change into something more "me." I could live again.

I want to make something clear. My mother is a good person, and she tried her best to make us kids feel loved, but when you are dealing with your own issues, it is hard to make other people feel OK when you are not. My mother is dealing with many of her own issues—issues that, as kids—we were not exposed to. I love my mother, and although our relationship is not where we would both like it to be all the time, I want the best for her and for her to be happy—just as I did when I was a kid. That will never change nor will the good times we have shared and the love I have for her in my heart. No one is perfect. I can attest to that, as I make many mistakes in my life, but as long as we try, and try to be our best, that is all we can ask for.

The conversation with my mom was tough. She did not want me to go. I am sure it hurt her very much, but I think deep down she knew it's what I needed. My mom is a good person. She has a big heart and has been there for me at many different transition points in my life, but she has also made me feel worse than I ever thought possible at times. She has put her feelings first and put her issues and scars on her kids, even though it was never intentional. It is sad because I know she had a rough childhood, but my hope has been and always will be for her to let it go and be happy. I just hope she continues to live in a way that makes her happy. I love my mom very much, but we are very different and see things differently, so it's hard sometimes. Back to the story, towards the end of the summer, I quit my job bagging groceries at Stew Leonard's and moved back to New York and in with my dad.

I loved playing sports. I have played competitive sports since I was a kid and all the way into my twenties and thirties, and now I coach both my sons' many sports teams. Track and field was my best sport, specifically the high jump, which I started in eighth grade after I moved in with my mom. Now, from eighth through tenth grade I was mediocre at best, never coming in first but always doing OK.

My confidence wasn't there in a lot of aspects of my life. It took more for me to truly live up to my potential, as you will see in the next chapter. Strategy Three integrates visual aids to help you transition, by looking at the new information in a positive way and recalling and relating the information to past experiences through illustration. The form of illustration in my story was a journal/writing, and it helped me build on Strategies One and Two through the transition of my parent's divorce.

Remember, we need to trust the process, as each sequential strategy builds on one another. This is how we ultimately succeed—we need to keep moving forward. Just as the process continues, so does our complex system of life. I may have pushed past the barriers with the divorce, but the underlying wounds (with insecurity and self-esteem) still remained and life at my mom's didn't help. My current therapist always says, if we pour salt on an open wound it will never heal, but if we let it scar up, then the salt will just fall off. I was ready to practice what I wanted in my heart. Strategy Four helps to continue through the transition process by utilizing practice or on-the-job training to succeed, building on what you have already accomplished with Strategies One through Three. It still blows me away how much my mindset changed when I moved in with my dad. He truly saved me and turned me into the man I am today, which is something I will never forget and hope to one day pass on to my boys.

CHAPTER SEVEN

Practice Makes Potential

Have you ever heard the saying, "Practice makes perfect?" Personally, I think that saying is bullshit. What is perfect anyway? How can we say that something is perfect (meaning flawless) but still admit we need improvement and practice? Perfect is an illusion. The minute we choose to stop learning is the minute we stop growing. This is especially true when it comes to transitional learning and PI. Remember, everything is a process—a continuous process that may need adjusting at times. Nothing is perfect. Perfection is something people strive for because they think that once it is attained they will feel fulfilled and be content with where they are and what they are working towards. Well, I can tell you, perfection is not all it is cracked up to be. I have perfected how to fail at times in my life, and it is not a place I like to be. No, a better way, at least in my opinion, is to say, "Practice makes potential." If we live up to our full potential, work hard to get to a place where we feel we have tried our best and are happy with the outcome, isn't that perfection? Just as transitions are specific to each individual, so are the outcomes achieved when they live up to their potential. Yes, practice makes potential. That's better.

This is a concept I try to portray to my boys every day. I feel like a broken record at times because, at their age, repetition is key! My boys are competitive and get frustrated when they do not win or do well. I make sure to tell them if they try hard and live up to their potential they have already won, and that's all Daddy cares about. My older son constantly says, "I know, Daddy, as long as I try my best, then you will be proud of me." It's hard being a parent and there is no playbook or instructions, so as a father, it's not always easy to find the line of being too hard on your kids or pushing them to their full potential. All I can do is continue to communicate with them and make sure they know I am always there to listen and to help them but also to push them to their full potential. Practice makes potential, so that is what we work on every day, whether it's with school, sports, or just being good for Mommy and Daddy.

Strategy Four builds on the previous three strategies. We have spent a good amount of time discussing receiving and perceiving the new information, recalling and relating examples, and implementing some form of illustration or visual aid to push through the barrier or obstacle we have encountered. Strategy Four now looks to practice what we preach, so to speak, and use the confidence and knowledge obtained and/or created during the first three strategies to persevere and be successful. Strategy Four is titled *Practicing and On-the-Job Training*, and it helps to identify new ideas for success and to relate the new ideas to existing information. You have outlined a solid base or framework of past experiences, both mentally and visually, and now it's time to expand your mindset and cognitive reach to identify new ideas and relate them with existing ones. This is primarily done through practice and student-centered learning—both observation and hands-on experiences. This type of exposure is key to success and increases your bandwidth for a favorable outcome. Implementing the ability to see the how-to of the tasks associated with the barrier, including recognition of mistakes, is imperative for success.

Observation can be an extremely helpful tool when working through an issue or trying to push past an obstacle or barrier. From the time we are small, we see something and try to mimic it. We learn by watching the people in our lives—first our family, then our friends, etc. We see things on television and at school, in our complex systems of life, that shape the way we see things and possibly the way we do things. This is why positive guidance and support is so imperative, regardless of age. We all need a push sometimes—some comments or words of encouragement that push us to be better. Hence, I constantly try to help my boys see this concept anytime they get frustrated or feel discouraged. I told you this book is not a textbook. It is a source of information and primarily a way to see how the strategies of success within the created TLP can be applied to everyday life and our complex system of life.

I have experienced a lifetime in forty-one years; I have seen things in my military career that have been extreme. I have lived and traveled all over the world and experienced things that have made me better—including things I never wish to see again. I have needed help at times, whether it be support from my family, friends, co-workers, or a therapist. Some things we have already discussed and some you will see later in this book. Strategy Four is the halfway point of the TLP process and brings us to about the halfway point in my life (or just a little shy of it). Remember, the strategies build on one another, and so do my experiences discussed in this book. This is my complex system of life and each experience has built on one another and made me the man I am today. Practice makes potential, and my experiences are no different. I have learned something from every one of them, good or bad.

After moving back in with my dad, I began transitioning to a place of comfort, where I hoped to find myself again and truly live up to my potential. I remember the day my dad came to pick me up, and we headed back to Staten Island. It was a sad moment leaving my mom, but I think we all knew this was what was best for me—and needed. I remember driving back, feeling happy, excited, and a little scared. I am a true New Yorker, inside and out, so I was excited to get back to New York and live in the city. My stepmom had set up the spare bedroom for me and even got me balloons and a *Welcome* sign. We went out to dinner at the Italian restaurant around the corner that I mentioned earlier in the book, and it all just felt right. After we went home, I got settled in, and the process to get me into the Catholic school my stepbrother was attending started. My grades were good, so getting accepted was not the problem, but once I went to orientation at the end of the summer, it hit me hard that I did not know anyone and had no friends to help me figure things out.

I was scared. I felt like that scared, intimidated kid who just left my mom's. The same sixteen-year-old kid who appeared shy and weak, and who was bullied by a bigger kid in the nineth grade. Yes, I was bullied, and it is something I do not wish on anyone. I just hope that bully has changed his ways by now, and knows bullying is a sign of weakness and insecurity (at least that's what I have read). During that time, I had little confidence and low self-esteem, and it didn't help that I was 120 pounds soaking wet. Now I was about to be a junior. I remember walking through the halls with the eleventh-grade class during orientation and watching all the kids who knew each other, who grew up with each other, and hung out together as they walked through, laughing and talking. I truly didn't know anyone, and I was not at a point where I felt confident enough to start up conversations. Besides, at sixteen, we all know how that goes. Not cool. I left orientation and headed home. We took city buses to school, so I recall standing on the bus thinking about what I was going to do. The first day of school came and went, and as expected, no one was beating the door down to let me into their crew. I was definitely intimidated and nervous, and I am sure it showed. I found a job at a grocery store, which I hated, but I did it to stay busy and because my dad told me I had to work. It wasn't until October of that year, two months into the school year that I started feeling better within the transition.

Sports was always something I could lose myself in. I grew up at a time when being outside was everything a kid wanted. Yeah, we played Nintendo and watched sitcoms and cartoons, but 90 percent of the time, we were outside. I have played sports since before I can remember, and it was always something that made me feel comfortable and helped me fit in. It took me a few weeks to figure out how things worked at school, but once they announced that the swim team was going to start practicing, I couldn't wait to sign up. As a kid, I played everything, but I excelled in track and field, football, and swimming. They used to call me Warner the Worm, and it stuck even into my adult years (for a different reason than with sports, though). I joined the swim team and things started to turn around. I began making friends, going to social functions, and having fun! I started breaking out of the shell that hardened while living at my mom's and started feeling like myself again. This continued into the track and field outdoor season, opening up more doors, friendships, and experiences. Something was happening within me as well —my confidence was increasing as I started feeling good about myself and my abilities.

This is where Strategy Four comes into play. This story focuses on my time on the track team and as a high jumper. Previously, the best I could do at the high jump was about five feet, four inches. This was not very high at all (borderline average). I was not sure why I had hit a wall with it, but honestly, I didn't think I was very good. I tried to perceive the information in a positive way but always felt defeated. I tried to Recall and Relate times when I did well or saw someone do well, and I even watched video tapes of myself and other jumpers. I applied the premise of the first three strategies, but Strategy Four was where I truly transitioned. This story shows just how important confidence is and how imperative it is to live up to your potential.

The season started out just as the one from my sophomore year; I was jumping with an average of around five feet, four inches. This continued for a bit, but two things had changed. First, I had a really good coach, a former high jumper, who helped me see different ways to be better and improve. Thanks Coach, I appreciate it more than words can say. Not just for the exercises but also for the guidance and support and for truly seeing my potential and helping me achieve it. This is where the second item came into play, confidence. My confidence started increasing as well.

I began practicing harder and harder, and it showed in more ways than one. I took the information I had, converted it into motivation, and worked harder than I had ever worked before. More importantly, I could feel it. I felt like I could do it, I had confidence in my abilities and felt like I was better than I let myself be. I watched videos, I watched other jumpers during meets, I practiced all of the tools and techniques I was taught and worked on them day in and day out. I felt alive and like I could succeed. I truly felt like I was living up to my potential, and it showed in my results. As the season went on, my confidence increased, and so did my performance. I began doing better and better and jumping higher and higher, and I was placing in meets. This is something I had never done before. I finished the season on a high note, placing first in the final meet with the highest jump of the day. I had gone from five feet, four inches, to five feet, ten inches by the end of the season. My coach and I had high hopes for my senior year, as I would compete in both the indoor and outdoor seasons.

My senior year I played football, was on the swim team, and competed in indoor and outdoor track and field. I also worked at a Genovese drug store about twenty hours a week and kept a B average at school. A typical day for me was school from about 7:30 a.m to 2:00 p.m. (I was a senior, so I got out a period early) and practice until about 4:30 p.m. every day. Then I went home, ate dinner, and headed to work from about 6:00 p.m. to 10 p.m. I would then come home and do school work for about an hour or two, go to bed, and do it all over again. For some of us, this seems normal. I am sure it is similar to what a lot of people did back then. I loved it! I tried to remain positive and push myself, just as the TLP encourages. I enjoyed the hard work and loved playing sports. So, after the football season, I began getting ready for the indoor track and field season. This was my time. I felt ready and couldn't wait to start.

I came out like a bullet, working hard and practicing, and it paid off. I don't know what happened to me during the transition between eleventh and twelvth grades, but I came out to my first track meet and jumped six feet—something I had never done. The harder I worked, the better I did, and it became the norm for me to jump six feet or higher during a meet. After a while, I wouldn't even come into the meet until the bar was at six feet. They would raise the bar to six feet, and there would only be a few people left. I would sail over the bar, no problem! I was at the top of my game and felt unstoppable—until I met my arch nemesis. I will leave his name out of it, but we'll call him Lex Luther (I am obviously Superman). Two skinny Catholic school boys who could raise the bar and the competition while battling it out with each other each meet. It came to a point when it was just him and me left, and we would battle it out each meet around six feet, four inches to see who was victorious. I remember looking through the Staten Island Advance every weekend and reading high school sports articles about me and Lex going back and forth. Now, I have to give credit where credit is due. He got the best of me on most occasions, as I stayed consistent at six feet, four inches to six feet, six inches. No matter how good I felt or did, he always seemed to get the better of me. I remember, at the Staten Island championship games, we were both at six feet, six inches, and I was actually winning on attempts. He pulled it out and took first as I could not get past six feet, six inches that week. We both qualified for the state championship that year, but he was not able to make it. It would have been nice to see us compete against one another at the highest level for a student athlete: the state championship.

I finished both the indoor and outdoor seasons with a personal record on all fronts. I exceeded all of my own expectations and lived up to my potential. I was good enough to even compete at the college level after graduation. I would not have been able to accomplish this without practice and hard work, but more importantly, remaining positive and confident in my transition. I observed, learned and worked hard, keeping a positive mindset and outlook, knowing in my heart the outcome would be what I expected and that I would succeed. This was very different from the way I looked at things the first four years I competed in the high jump. The transition point occurred for me when I moved in with my dad, but it opened the door to numerous transitions, including living up to my full potential at sports, specifically the high jump.

Years after graduation, my father used to tell me he would look at the paper every week, and he never saw anything like what was reported about Superman and Lex (me and my oppenent that is). He said he never saw two guys go at it like us. I remember laughing when he said that but feeling good inside because I knew how hard I worked. Recently, my wife, my step-daughter, and I were talking about my glory days back in high school. Well, they were busting my chops about it actually. We looked up my high school and were surprised to see that one of my school records still exists in the track and field archive. Over twenty years later, I'm still printed in the record books. I couldn't believe it. It's something we joke about to each other, but it would not have been possible without hard work and confidence. I had some pretty amazing teammates, many who succeeded, and we all raised each other's game by working hard. Remember, practice makes potential, and it shows when you believe in yourself, remain confident, and (most importantly) remain positive about the outcome.

Strategy Four focuses on practice and working through the different aspects of on-the-job training. My example looks at a positive experience of practice and hard work. There are all different forms of practice, both good and bad. We see negative examples just as much, and even practice in negative ways at times. The goal is that we recognize this and make sure we use it as a practice of what not to do. Practice can come in any form of what we see, what we do, what we are taught, and what we are exposed to. In my entire career competing, I was exposed to good and bad examples, times when my transitions were positive and negative. I pulled back from my potential at times and worked hard to my full level of potential at times. I was confident at times and not so confident at times. The great thing about practicing what we preach is that we can do what we know is right—based on what we know is wrong. It is truly up to us how we want to live and how we want to practice. The truth is, only we know our true potential in life, only we know what we are capable of in our complex system, and what outcome we truly want to achieve. Sometimes it just takes practice.

When I applied Strategy Four to my life, I excelled and succeeded. I took the components associated with practice and accomplished my full potential at levels I never thought possible for myself. Practice makes potential, and it changed my life; it helped me see just how much success is possible. Remember, it's all a process, and we need to trust the process. When we break obstacles and barriers down into manageable steps, success is possible. That's what these strategies do if you have not noticed yet. It breaks down your reaction to the obstacle during your transition into steps, attacking them in different ways, with the ultimate goal of succeeding and pushing through the transition. I competed in track and field from nine years old until I was about twenty-two. I competed in high school, college, and in the military, and I did so at my full potential once I let myself. I succeeded in my eyes.

Now, during that time, I did have some help along the way. I had people guide me, support me, teach me, and most importantly, provide me with constructive criticism when I needed it. They gave me feedback, and I returned it with either my performance or a question. Strategy Five looks at how we can apply the different forms of feedback within our transition process—to help us be better and push past the obstacle or barrier we are facing in our transition. Some people do not like feedback, as they believe it to be negative in nature. Most of the time, it tells us what we are doing wrong and where we need to improve. The truth is, it is not always negative, and it is meant to help us be better, help us succeed. Just as we need to receive the new information in a positive way in Strategy One, we need to do the same with feedback in Strategy Five: view feedback in a positive way. Do you see the pattern here I am getting at? I hope so! Our complex system of life is just that, complex, so we need to have an open mind and see our different transitions in a positive way. If we do this, we are already ahead of the power curve. Practice makes potential, and it continues with feedback.

CHAPTER EIGHT

Thanks for the Feedback!

Think about a time when you were listening to someone provide you with information—whether good or bad—and your first instinct was to think about it in a negative way. I am sure you can all relate to this; I know there have been many instances where I have done this—especially when I was receiving one of my dad's infamous lectures about respect and showing respect, or some shit like that. I went into each of these with the same mentality: again! As kids, this is a pretty normal reaction, but as we evolve in our thinking and in the way we perceive things in our complex system of life, we are able to grow and think outside the box. Now, as a father myself, I can see that my dad was trying to portray an idea of respect for us, which is something I continue to attempt with my own kids. I shy away from the lengthy lectures but understand where he was coming from and what he was trying to say. The issue with this form of feedback is that it is often a give-and-no-take scenario.

Feedback can either be provided or received, and the difference between the two is the path to your overall outcome. Let me explain. If you are in a situation where it is clear that you will not have an opportunity to provide a response or feedback of your own, the opposing party is most likely going to instantly see this as a negative interaction—similar to how I felt during one of my dad's lectures. There was no opportunity for me to respond or truly reflect on what he was saying; it just felt like he was talking down to me. The same goes when you are providing feedback to someone. If you just talk at people and don't implement the idea that they will have an opportunity to respond or react, then their mentality or mindset will sway towards the negative. This goes back to the cognitive approach discussed earlier; it looks at how we think, how we learn, and how we perceive information. This is why feedback is such an important tool within communication and transitional learning.

I want you to think about what feedback means to you. Think about a time when you received feedback and a time when you provided it. Was it two-way feedback or one-way feedback? Did it help or hinder both the relationship and your success? Now, think about Strategies One through Four and how each provided a new step in the process of working through your specific transition. Remember, this is a sequential process and each strategy builds on one another. We have now approached the midpoint of the process. We are at a point in our transition where we have perceived the new information in a positive way, we have recalled examples and related them to things we know, we have used visual aids in the form of illustrations and/or text to help us push through the transition and understand, and we have practiced and worked to our full potential though hands-on experiences or observations to continue to work through the transition in question in our complex system of life. All strategies to this point have focused on our own positive viewpoints, our own steps within the process where we are in the driver's seat. Everything is a process, and we are now at a pivotal point in the process where we look to external sources for further understanding and clarification; it's time to institute feedback platforms.

Even when feedback is constructive and discusses ways you can improve, it should still be perceived in a positive way. It mirrors the ideas we see in Strategy One, as we need to perceive the feedback with a positive outlook so we can truly process and reflect on what is being provided. The first four strategies in the process work through the transition internally, building confidence with a positive outlook. The remaining four strategies implement external methods for success within the process, with feedback being the first. Feedback does not always feel good or seem beneficial; we are predetermined to get defensive and react according to our emotions when it is constructive, but if we go into it with a positive mindset, knowing that it is meant to help us and not hurt us, then we are already on the right track.

Let me clarify a bit. Not all information being presented to you is feedback. When I discuss feedback, I am referring to actual feedback—information being presented during an interaction that is helping the recipient or providing the recipient with constructive ideas on how to improve on performance or in understanding. Leadership expert Ken Blanchard coined the phrase, "Feedback is the breakfast of champions because without a regular serving of feedback, you are likely to starve." The bottom line, or main point I am trying to make, is that feedback is something we can learn from, it is information we can build and improve on, whether good or bad, but it all depends on how we perceive it, and ultimately, that we can not progress without it.

I can tell you, in my complex system of life, when I have received feedback in a positive way, it has really made a difference. I can't say it enough, if we break things down into manageable steps, then anything is possible. This is extremely evident when receiving and providing feedback, as it will assist in opening our minds to see things we may not initially see. We all need help and guidance at times, and the TLP is meant to assist us with that. The great thing about feedback is that once we utilize it, whether provided or received, we can implement it into future endeavors when we encounter a similar obstacle or barrier. There are all different transitions in our complex system of life, each with a different path, but just as we Recall and Relate information in Strategy Two, we can also apply feedback in this manner to current and future transitions.

Feedback can also do wonders for an individual's confidence, as it can provide a newfound sense of worth in your abilities when you have the opportunity to voice your concerns. The application of feedback can build confidence in both your level of knowledge and of understanding, as you can institute your own connections to current processes, and any new processes you encounter. Remember, it can benefit future endeavors just as much as your current transitions. Strategy Five represents its own transition point within the process, as it shifts focus to external factors in connection with the internal factors we see in Strategies One through Four. Strategy Five, titled

Instituting Feedback and Collaboration, provides the ability to add new ideas to existing ones by receiving or providing feedback in a positive way.

The next experience I want to reference looks at a time in my life when I was at a major pivotal transition point. It is from about the halfway point in my life to date, which makes sense, as we are at the halfway point in the process. It was during a time where I was transitioning quite a bit, as I was experiencing college life and being on my own for the first time. Most of the examples provided to this point have more of a serious premise base, so let's lighten things up a bit. This experience looks at the way feedback can be received and applied to current and future transitions and how it can truly change how you see and do things. It's humorous and enjoyable but memorable for me, to say the least.

During the discussion for Strategy Four, you saw how I ended my high school track and field career on a high note. Practice makes potential, and I wasn't going to stop pushing forward. So, when I left for college, I had high hopes for success. Yeah, I was nervous, but it was more of an excited nervous feeling, similar to the feeling I felt when I moved back in with my dad. I attended orientation over the summer and connected with people in my dorm and in the same major. I did pretty well in math in high school, and my aspirations to become an engineer was still there, so I chose to major in mathematics. Big mistake! College level calculus is not the same as high school sequential math, and I found that out pretty quickly. I started my freshman year with an open mind, ready for whatever challenges came my way. I figured I would compete in track and field, study, hang with friends, and so on. I was really excited about what was coming. Oh yeah, did I mention I had never partied like that before? I was all about sports in high school, so I was not ready for all that college had to offer, as I had only been drunk a handful of times at that point. It took about two days before I was fully engulfed in the extracurricular activities of college, which consisted of drinking underage, going out, and living the college dream. I felt like I was on top of the world. My original expectations for what college would be began to fade, quickly.

My freshman year was a blur, as I pledged an unsanctioned fraternity, drank to the point of getting alcohol poisoning, and partied about six nights a week. It was a pretty exciting year for a young freshman, and I lived it up. I managed to hold a GPA hovering around 2.0, which I thought was OK, but my dad did not. I didn't realize just how bad that was until later in life but that's a whole different story. I felt confident going into sophomore year, at least with the social aspects of college. Oh yeah, I forgot to mention—I competed on the track and field team for a bit, quitting after about two months because it interfered with my party time (yes, very stupid decision). So, on a social level, I was ready to go.

Sophomore year started on a high note. My fraternity pretty much ran the school social scene. We had a ridiculous house and amazing parties, and some of my closest friends and I all lived in one of the suites on campus. Man, the stories I could tell you are both humorous and scary—but very entertaining. Actually, I recently started a production company with three of these guys I am talking about, and we have created a pretty amazing television series titled "Cowbirds," which is based on different aspects of attending college in the late '90s. It is both funny and dramatic; as it shows the dark side of college life in an unsanctioned fraternity as well as the funny and memorable times of four friends from Staten Island. This is a fictional show but is loosely based on our exeriences. We are actually in the process of pitching it during the publication of this book, so check out Buddy Buddy Productions, LLC and www.cowbirds.com for additional information. The sky's the limit, as the Notorious B.I.G stated in a popular '90s rap song. The music during that time was like no other, to me, it was an introduction to hip-hop unlike we had seen. The bars pumped it, and you couldn't help but dance. This is where I got the adult version of the nickname Warner the Worm. The boys knew they could always count on me to do The Worm on the bar on any given night. I am known for The Worm and fake falls—my legacy so to speak. Of course, I am kidding, but those were definite staples on any given night.

Sophmore year, a few of us decided to take an Introduction to Management course. It was the first business course I had taken in college. Most of my freshman year was geared toward general education requirements and math courses. By this point I knew that was not the direction I wanted to go, so I felt good when I registered for the management course, as it could provide me with some direction and maybe a different career plan. So, a bunch of us decided to take this management course, which was a lecture course in a typical college lecture hall.

About a month into the course, we were instructed to form groups of four or five. Then the instructor would assign our group a topic for discussion. Each group would develop a presentation on the topic, and each member would be required to present a portion to the class and the professor. I have to admit, I was a little intimidated. I had never done anything like this before, and I wasn't sure how it would turn out. I was at a transition point and not sure how to push past the barrier in front of me. Our group got the topic of discrimination in the workplace, and the four of us decided to each pick a different form of discrimination that may present itself in the workplace. The four subtopics we decided upon were gender, ethnicity, race, and age. My assignment was age discrimination, and I had no clue about how I was going to do it.

The four of us worked hard putting together a pretty good report and presentation, at least we thought so. But, still, we each needed to present our own portion, which meant getting up in front of the class and professor and discussing our subtopic. I was nervous, but volunteered to go first. I wanted to kick things off, as I felt it was better to be first than last; the class's attention is usually higher in the beginning, right? I got my index cards ready (do people still use these?) and was ready to go. Remember, computers were just starting to hit the scene as a tool, so we went old school and used a projector and flash cards. I remember putting my portion together the day before, thinking about the best way to present. I took the new information, thought about presentations I could Recall and Relate to, laid out the different visual aids we created, and practiced my pitch so to speak.

I like to laugh and be funny—I feel laughter is the true key to happiness. I believe that bringing humor to any situation decreases tension and helps people relax and be themselves. I did not want to be a stiff (someone who just reads off of cards and does not provide entertainment). People want to be entertained, and I believe if you bring humor to a presentation, it helps people engage and be involved in the content. In my view, the best course of action would be to make it funny. I thought about how to do this in a way where my buddies and the class would be entertained, but the professor would also be intrigued and interested. People can smell confidence, it's like blood in the water, and if you come in there intimidated or not confident, you are already behind the power curve. The four of us met before class and discussed the project. I informed the team that my goal was to make them and the class laugh at my presentation and gave them some insight into my execution. They didn't believe me—crazy, right? Well, just an FYI, they were happily surprised and pleased with my performance.

Remember, I chose to take the lead, so I needed to set the bar high. C'mon, what did I have to lose? The content was there, so I knew we checked all the boxes. It was now time to execute and deliver. Our group was the second group to go for that class. I could already see the eyes of the students beginning to gloss over, so I needed to hit a homerun. The professor was sitting in the first row on the end, so she was front and center. She called our team, and we proceeded to the front of the classroom and set up our papers on the projector. (Man, it's crazy to think how we used to do things back then compared to now.) Here we go, all setup and ready. My team stood to the side with half smiles on their face, awaiting what was to come. I remember a sense of excitement and nervousness coming over me. I had a small bead of sweat on my upper lip, hands a bit clammy, but ready to go. I took a breath and started the presentation. I stood there, looked at the silent class, and stated:

"Age discrimination....what is...(long pause)... age discrimination?"

I used animated mannerisms and witty comments which raised giggles. I could hear students from the back row. I continued to bring humor to the presentation by moving toward the professor, who was sitting on the corner of the desk, and directing questions and comments directly to her. She seemed interested, while my team and the rest of the class tried their best not to laugh. I looked at her and said, "Professor, why is this a problem in the workplace? I'll tell you why." (Finger in the air and everything).

I could see my team from the corner of my eye, turned away, red-faced, trying not to laugh out loud. I felt alive and comfortable, and the remaining few minutes flew by as each of us had five minutes to present. When my portion was complete, I handed the baton to my teammate, and we killed the rest of the presentation. The tension was gone, and my entire team succeeded. The class clapped at the end of the presentation, and my team told me how ridiculous I was and how funny it was. I was happy about the outcome and thought I did amazing, with no issues. Well, just as we discussed earlier in the chapter, the feedback you receive is not always the feedback you expect. The instructor provided us with open feedback but did not specifically mention anything about my comedic masterpiece. I decided to go to her office hours the next day and obtain my accolades as an amazing presenter. That is not what happened. I am sure you can imagine.

I remember approaching her office with high confidence, ready for my feedback. I knocked on the door, and she motioned me to come in and sit down. I told her I wanted to discuss my presentation, and she said she was happy I came by, as she wanted to speak with me about it. I knew it. Here it comes. She looked at and said, "I think it could have been better." I sat there stunned. I was not expecting that and truly did not know how to respond. I think she could see the confusion on my face because she followed up with, "Don't get me wrong. I am not saying it was bad at all. I just feel like it could have been executed a bit better." I felt all of the confidence drain from my body. See what happens when you perceive the information in a negative way? All I heard was it could have been better. It didn't even dawn on me to see the positive side and actually engage and respond to the comments. I took a minute and sat in silence. The professor must be familiar with the concepts behind Strategy Five because she knew how to help me engage. She simply asked me my thoughts. I took a breath and proceeded to provide her with my own feedback about my presentation and her comments. My professor helped me to see the benefits of being funny and instituting humor but also underscored the need for regulation and balance with the other aspects of the presentation. It's all about balance—something that is truly evident in every aspect of life and in each of our own complex systems.

We chatted and communicated back and forth for about forty-five minutes, and she went over the pros and cons of my presentation and what I could do better. She made me see that bringing humor and one's own personality traits is vital to success, and she encouraged me to build on what I started. She helped me see how to balance this, and honestly, it is something I have continued to try and master in any presentation I have ever done. I decided to receive the feedback in a positive way (and to provide feedback myself—to help push through my transition of becoming a better presenter). I have been doing this for over twenty years, in the classroom, at work, in the military, and in other endeavors where I am required to present. It all started with instituting feedback in the correct way and applying the new information to my current processes and transitions. The next "presentaion based" course I took was public speaking, requiring four presentations. I had a great instructor who continued to help me as I applied the feedback received during my management course and I could feel my confidence increasing.

I know that I continue to discuss the process and how we need to trust the process, but this is just another example of how important it is to build on each strategy with the goal of transitioning successfully. Each strategy builds on one another, and in order for success to be possible, each stage in the process needs to be implemented. Strategy Five is the first transition where external factors play a significant role, but each of the first four strategies need to be applied for the TLP to work its magic. That is the beauty of the process: once each manageable step or strategy is accomplished, overall success is not far behind. Once feedback is both received and applied, we are ready to be put to the test and see how prepared we are to overcome the obstacle and push through the transition.

I want you to think about a time when feedback played a significant role in your life. Think about your initial reactions and your mindset. Were you opposed to the feedback or did you welcome it? Think about how you felt, how you reacted, and what the overall outcome was? Now think about what you could have changed. Think about what has been discussed with Strategy Five and how you could have applied the ideas and concepts of Strategy Five to that instance. I want you to truly reflect on how Strategy Five could have played a role? Up to this point, we have received the new information and maintained a positive outlook throughout. We have related and recalled examples we are familiar with to help understand the information, and we have implemented visual aids for further comprehension, practiced and received feedback. Now it's time for us to evaluate our abilities in regard to the transition. Strategy Six continues with the theme of external factors and administers the test and evaluation phase of the process. It's all a process, and we need to trust the process.

CHAPTER NINE

This is Only a Test...

Isn't it funny how we can feel so confident in our abilities but tense up when we know we are being evaluated or formally tested? I have always been a fan of the idea behind informal testing—where you are being tested but don't know you are being tested. Man, I wish that was really a thing. I bet I would do fantastic. Most people's anxiety and stress levels increase when they know they are being evaluated or tested (even if they just scored high on a practice test with the same information). It's just the *knowing* that you are being tested that brings all types of negative cognitive thoughts and reactions. Remember the perceptions we discussed in the beginning of this book? Remember that I continued to talk about being positive and looking at things in a positive way with an open mind? Well, tests and evaluations are no different. We need to remember one important aspect when we are evaluated—it's only a test! Most of us have probably seen or heard the infamous test of the Emergency Broadcast System. Normally, it occurs around three in the morning during an infomercial about some new cleaning product, but it's a sound we will never forget, like nails on a chalkboard. "This is only a test." Anytime I am being evaluated, I take a deep breath and think about this unforgettable sound and saying. Remember, no matter what the outcome—it is only a test.

    I haven't always been able to do this. I will be honest, I used to be just as susceptible as the next person to the stress and anxiety of being evaluated. I started sweating and had that nervous feeling, thinking the worst, and hoping for the end to come. I couldn't sleep the night before and thought about every which way to get out of it. Think about how much time, mental anguish, and pressure that puts on a person. I want you to think about a time when this happened to you. C'mon, we have all been there. Think about a time when you were being evaluated and all of the above was going on inside you. Put yourself back to how you were feeling, your mindset, and the way you reacted. Were you focusing on the positive? Were you feeling confident? Did you look at it like a test or the end of all time? Don't worry, we have all been there.

Now, compare this to just telling yourself it is only a test and that you will do the best you can. A big difference, right? I am not sure when and how my shift in thinking occurred, but I started looking at testing and evaluating in a positive way—as a transition point where I can learn, enhance my abilities, become better, and ultimately be successful. Manageable steps—that is the key. If we break things down into manageable steps and approach each step with confidence and positivity, our chances for success are so much higher. This is never an easy thing to do, especially when we are being evaluated, but really think about it. Is there a better way to test our abilities or understanding of the new information within the transition, short of working through the barrier or obstacle in a real time, real world instance? Evaluations are our chance to shine and show our stuff, so to speak, before we are put in a position where it really matters. This is only a test, remember.

Isn't that what testing and evaluating is meant to do? Strategy Six does just that. It is the point in the transition process where we administer tests and evaluations as a means for success—to elaborate on the content being processed throughout the previous strategies within the TLP and review the results through feedback and communication. Remember, it's a process and we need to trust the process. Strategy Six provides the individual with a platform to show what they have learned, recalled, illustrated, practiced, and received feedback on. The test or evaluation is not a chance to fail but a chance to shine and show your stuff. Isn't that a better way to look at it? You may not meet the expectations or requirements of the evaluation and have to retest or be reevaluated but doesn't it ultimately make you better at what you're trying to do? The more we practice, receive feedback, and test ourselves, the better we will be, and the more successful we will ultimately become.

It may not feel this way all the time, as it feels pretty crummy when we do not pass or are unable to meet the requirement, but this is just another transition point and a chance to look at things positively. The evaluation does not prove we are not good enough but only addresses any inconsistencies we may have demonstrated through feedback and collaboration so that we can be successful when we are required to accomplish the task in a real time situation. In regard to the TLP and Strategy Six, administering tests and evaluations are meant to enhance positivity in the mentor/trainee relationship. It is meant to implement realism into the training or execution of training to ultimately make sure the employee is ready when expected to execute the task during real time events. Strategy Six is ultimately a platform for success, and if we look at it as just a test, the outcome will only increase our chances of success when the time comes for action, or when you are expected to execute for real.

One of the major benefits of tests and evaluations is that they are different from training or practicing, as they put the individual in the driver's seat and give them the opportunity to showcase their skills. They provide realism versus simulation. They are the closest thing to a realistic scenario and what you will see real time. They provide a realistic measure of how the individual may perform when required, whether in life, at school, at work, or in my case—during military operations. I personally believe this is why I was able to ultimately apply the ideas within Strategy Six in a positive way to any evaluation or test I have been involved with in the military. Honestly, there have been times in my career—when it could have meant life or death—that evaluations provided me with a chance to enhance my abilities and prepare.

During the chapter on Strategy Five, we discussed instituting feedback into the process. Once feedback is instituted, Strategy Six (next in the sequence) is your chance to administer tests and evaluations to measure your level of understanding and possible outcomes for success. That is the beauty of this process—it injects the ideas behind continuous learning, where each strategy can be reapplied and/or executed again, to enhance the individual's chances for success and ability to transition through the obstacle or barrier in front of them. The TLP can be applied to any transition within our complex system of life, and each appilcation will only strengthen your understanding of it and of how to apply and execute each strategy and ultimately be successful. It's about being the best version of yourself, living up to your potential, and being successful.

Another aspect of testing and evaluation that I want to discuss is the idea that everyone tests differently. Just as we all learn differently and may need a different cognitive approach than someone else, the same goes for testing. It is the job of the evaluator to know their people, and understand the student's strengths and weaknesses. This doesn't mean the requirements change, but it is beneficial to an evaluator and the individual being evaluated to execute the examination in a way where the individual can feel comfortable and be successful. This is why feedback and communication are vital to the process. It is a way for each individual in the process to get to know one another, what works, and what can be changed or adjusted. This can be the deciding factor for success and will only benefit each party involved. This will most likely affect the levels of confidence of the individual being evaluated. It honestly depends on how the test or evaluation is administered. Trust me, I can tell you first hand, that when Strategy Six is applied in the proper way, building on Strategies One through Five, success is possible. I am not saying you will always meet the requirement, but you will do better if you look at it in a positive way, and it will help you continue to succeed in the future. If we break things down into manageable steps, it increases our chances for success. It will ultimately increase our confidence and help us to be ready when it matters.

The experience I want to discuss in regards to Strategy Six not only looks at administering tests and evaluations, but it shows how they can increase confidence and help you succeed, when viewed in a positive way. Members of the military are required to complete an initial evaluation to become certified in their given position. When I joined the military, I went to basic training in the Open-General category, which meant I would be assigned whatever job met the needs of the USAF. I was not comfortable letting my fate be determined by something else, and I was not sure how long I would be serving in the military, so I wanted to have a job that I enjoyed. I had initially signed for four years but was not sure at that time if I was going to make a career out of it. I knew I wanted to serve my country, as I have always felt a desire to serve something higher than myself, so this was exactly where I needed to be. Open-General meant I did not know what job I would get, so while in basic training, I explored other avenues, which led me to TACP.

My first duty station was Würzburg, Germany, which is unreal to a twenty-two-year-old kid from New York City. I remember getting off the plane with my V-neck T-shirt, visor, and silver chain, wondering where I was. I found out later that the dude picking me up thought the same thing when he saw this NYC Guido coming his way. He could already hear the, "How you doing" greeting coming from my mouth. My first year in Germany was unbelievable. I met some awesome guys—some of them I consider family (especially my buddies Shawn and Justin). They are truly my brothers and have helped me at times, and in ways, that I appreciate to a level I cannot portray in words. Love you, brother! I was loving life, succeeding at work, increasing my level of culture and travel, and making connections that would last a lifetime. I was truly living the dream. I was learning a lot about my chosen career, as well, and loving every minute of it. As mentioned, a TACP is a forward air controller who is attached to their assigned and supported Army unit, providing air coverage during peacetime and combat operations. Pretty much, it's the guy who drops the bombs when shit hits the fan, with the infamous words, "You're cleared hot." It's a pretty bad ass job, and one that I was happy to be a part of.

Now, you do not become a certified controller, which is a certified Joint Terminal Attack Controller, or JTAC, overnight. It takes a few years to become certified, and your rite of passage is becoming a subject matter expert on the radios and equipment, acting as your JTAC's radio operator first. The TACP team consists of a radio operator maintainer and driver (ROMAD), or radio bitch, and a JTAC, who is the lead controller and the dude who drops the bombs. To become a certified ROMAD, you need to pass your initial evaluation and be signed off. I completed this feat (hungover might I add) by the end of my first year in Germany. This is the first step to becoming a certified JTAC (which was ETAC back then, for all my old heads). I was at a point when I could sit back, continue to learn and work hard, and begin working on my individual development, such as professional development and college courses. Things were going great, and I felt good about where I was, powering through my transitions with success. This was in June of 2002, so 9/11 had recently occurred and the tempo was increasing, preparing me for what was next.

I will never forget where I was when the 9/11 attacks occurred. I joined the military in 2000 (so before 9/11). It is crazy to think how, in this coming September after publication of this book, twenty years will have passed since the attacks. I had been in Germany for two months at this point and was at a field exercise. I remember sitting in the HUMVEE working on the radios when people started running around screaming that everyone had to get back to the main base. We were literally living in the field, training on different aspects of the job. I was asking questions on our way back to the main base, but no one really knew what was going on. Once we got back to the main base, we entered the building where everyone had gathered; it was the first time I saw the horrendous effects of that horrific day. People did not know what to do or how to feel or react. I remember hearing one young soldier yell at another soldier who was getting a haircut. He said, "How can you be getting a haircut right now? We are going to war." It seemed a little humorous at the time, but hey, everyone reacts differently. The next three days were a blur. The base was locked down and to make matters worse, I could not get anyone on the phone back in New York to make sure my family and friends were OK. It took me three days to get in touch with my dad, who fortunately told me everyone in our family was OK. This was not the case for everyone and was not the case for some people I know. My heart goes out to them and their families.

I am sure you can imagine what the military tempo was like during that time. I will not go into details, but it was no secret. We were preparing. At that point in my career, I was working toward my ROMAD certification and ultimately my JTAC certification. I spent two years in Germany, from 2001 to 2003, preparing and getting ready for my time to shine. As you know from previous chapters, my first deployment was in 2002-2003. I was part of the team that invaded Iraq during Operation Iraqi Freedom. I was a ROMAD, so my job was focused on the radios and equipment. I met a lot of really great fellow TACP's during that time, and it was a deployment filled with many memories, some good and some not so good, but all of them represent a time I will never forget. I was part of something pretty amazing, and it felt good to serve something higher than myself.

After I left Germany, I was stationed at Fort Riley, Kansas. Imagine having to go from Germany to Kansas. Nothing against Kansas, but it was definitely a shock. The good thing was I knew a few of the guys stationed there; one I had just been deployed with. I even moved in with him when I got to Fort Riley, and we were roommates during my two years there. He also helped me during one of the hardest times of my life, and I will never forget that. Thanks, Buddy—or, as we called him, "Yuk Mouth." Love ya, brother. When I got to Fort Riley, I was a Senior Airmen (E-4) and primed and ready to become a JTAC. I had completed two ROMAD evaluations, a deployment, and logged numerous practice controls (that is controlling aircraft) on the path to getting my initial

JTAC evaluation. You needed so many practice controls—different types—before you could have your initial JTAC certification. This included live controls with live ordinance on a bombing range, laser guided controls, dry controls, night controls, etc. The trips to the range, called Close Air Support (CAS) trips, were something else. Put aside the comradery developed, there is nothing like watching an A-10 warthog give you a panel check on top of an observation point (OP). It truly is surreal.

So, in March of 2004, I was ready. I had all of my training completed, I attended all the required schools, and I had all of my practice controls logged and graded. This is one of the things I loved about the military and specifically the TACP career field. Everything was hands on. There was very little classroom training after technical school. Most training was accomplished in the field or at a CAS range. A typical day for us young ROMAD's was loading up the HUMVEE with equipment, grabbing a 1098 training form, and heading out to the field. Let me clarify what I mean by equipment. Yes, we grabbed radios and field training equipment, but it also meant grabbing the grill and cooler filled with drinks, meat, and condiments. It would have been nice if I meant beers, but no, water and soda. Still, we would head out to the field, complete some training items and sign them off on the 1098, then grill and bullshit (possibly take a nap), and finish the day putting the HUMVEE's to the test. How can you not love that job! We were preparing for war; a TACP's job is completed during combat. Training was our way of preparing, and as long as it got done, our superiors did not ask questions. It was a pretty awesome time, and I was ready for the next step of becoming a JTAC.

The day was sunny and warm. It was March in Kansas (just past the bitter cold time). I was told a week earlier that my evaluation would be at the local bombing range and conducted by our chief instructor. I was friendly with him on a social level, so I already felt comfortable. At that time, the TACP career field was not very big and everyone knew everyone, so we were all pretty close. I remember I was so excited. I was nervous but ready. I spent the week preparing. This was a transition point for me, and I was not looking at it negatively, as this was what all ROMAD's wanted to become. By this point in my career I had perceived the new information positively, I reviewed and recalled experiences of other certified JTAC's, I wrote notes and viewed imagery and other visual aids, I practiced and worked hard, I listened to feedback and was ready for my chance to shine. This was the evaluation stage, the second external factor in the TLP process. I was ready to apply Strategy Six, administering tests and evaluations to elaborate on previous content discussed, observed, and reviewed. My

ROMAD and I loaded the vehicle for our navigation to the range, I pulled my crisp black beret tight on my head, got out my map, and we headed out.

An initial evaluation to become a certified JTAC is not short. It can take a few hours to complete; there are numerous parts to accomplish. I have not been a member of the career field since 2014, so I am sure things have changed at this point. My first evaluation was in 2004, so I am sure things are different now. I am discussing my first experience with becoming a JTAC, I am sure each controller has their own. I broke each requirement down into manageable steps and trusted the process, which worked well for me and helped me succeed. Remember to trust the process. I was ready for everything the instructor threw at me, and worked to the full level of my potential and ability. I remember wondering at times if I had made any mistakes but quickly pushed past that thinking and continued forward. TACP are familiar with a specific saying, "The strong shall stand, and the weak will fall by the wayside." Damn right, and I was not about to let my curiosities and perceptions lead me to the wayside. I finished the evaluation and was told that I had passed and was a certified JTAC.

I still get chills thinking about it. I was so happy and felt on top of the world. My instructor provided me with feedback, including things I could work on, which I was more than happy to listen to and apply in the future. He even told me that it was the best initial evaluation he had done, and it made me feel great, as my hard work had paid off. I worked through the process, and applied the concepts associated with Strategies One through Five to help me accomplish Strategy Six—being successful in my evaluation. I was now a certified JTAC and ready to show what I had accomplished in combat. With the tempo being as high as it was, I knew I would soon be deploying again, and I was ready. There is nothing like accomplishing a goal, especially when you know you have given it your all. It's pretty amazing to say the least.

To this point in the TLP, we have discussed Strategies One through Six, which have culminated with an evaluation of abilities to push through the transition. Strategy Seven and Eight expand on understanding the concepts associated with the barrier or obstacle within the transition, as they apply problem-solving techniques and support systems to the process to assist in your success. Strategy Seven is titled *Applying Problem Solving Techniques* and looks at difficult scenarios or situations where an improvement can occur. I spent about another four months at Fort Riley, and then was approved to transition from active duty to the Air National Guard. I wanted to finish college with the hope of becoming an officer, and I felt this was my best path to do that. Little did I know, I would deploy just as much in the guard as I would have on active duty. I arrived at my guard unit in June of 2004 and was quickly informed of a deployment the following March of 2005. It was a division-level deployment in Iraq, so no field time. It wasn't until I returned home from that deployment and volunteered for a deployment to Afghanistan in 2006 that I got to see action in combat as a JTAC that you wouldn't believe. You know the saying, beware of what you wish for—well, my wish came true, and it was a deployment I will never forget. It is also where I was able to apply the next strategy—Strategy Seven, which helps us apply problem-solving techniques to our transitions. Remember, each strategy is sequential, building on those previous, and this was the next transition in my life where I needed to trust the process, as it could have truly meant my life.

CHAPTER TEN

The Solution Isn't Always Simple

Wouldn't it be nice if all solutions to every problem were laid out in front of us like a playbook, with a defensive or offensive strategy for every play or encounter? The reality, within our complex system of life, is that we encounter things that we are not expecting and do not know how to deal with. The TLP strategies for success were created to help us address these different encounters and create a positive solution to a barrier or obstacle we may face during a transition. Strategy Seven specifically focuses on the proper course of action; it applies problem-solving techniques to the barrier or obstacle being addressed within the transition. Think about a Rubik's Cube. I may be dating myself, but this was a challenge as a kid that I still have trouble with. Deployed members of the military always find toys, games, or other items left behind to play with. I have been known to pick one of these up and give it a shot, with little success. I have tried to accomplish this feat a handful of times, but am still waiting for my time to shine.

The process of applying problem-solving techniques is similar to working through the transition of attempting a Rubik's Cube. There are many different directions or courses of action available, but ultimately, one works best for the given situation. You may fail throughout the process, but this will help to show you the direction not to go and what does not work on the road to victory. As we continue to say, we need to remain positive in order to achieve success; we will only succeed if we push forward and work through the barrier or obstacle within our transition. Life is full of solutions, some good, some bad, some work, some don't. The goal is to keep an open mind and remain positive, as it is very easy to lose confidence and hope when techniques we apply do not work—just as we see with the Rubik's Cube.

Trust the process. I am sure you are sick of hearing this by now, but it works. We need to remain positive and trust the process, and we will ultimately be successful in our attempt. Remember, manageable steps. It's all a process, and this is very much the case with Strategy Seven. Applying problem-solving techniques means utilizing the proper course of action to work through the transition and its associated barriers or obstacles. The solution is not always simple. There are a few steps we can take when applying problem-solving techniques. Four specific steps, when followed, will help in working through Strategy Seven. They are:

- creating a list of courses of action
- analyzing the courses of action
- selecting the proper course of action
- applying the course of action or problem solving technique to the transition

Strategies One through Six have brought us to a point in the process where we feel internally confident in our abilities and continue to apply external factors to the process. We are at a crossroads.

Put yourself in this scenario. You are driving down the highway and come to a fork in the road—but it's more of a T intersection, actually, where you can go one way and experience all it has to offer or go the opposite way and experience all that way has to offer. The problem is that your map has been destroyed, and your smartphone has no service for GPS. You truly have no clue what the right direction is. You are packed, have a full tank of gas, food, and water and you are prepared. You remain positive and feel confident in your abilities. You have seen instances like this before and can recall examples from memory; you have also seen this in movies and on TV. You have simulated this experience in your mind before the trip and practiced what you would do. Have you noticed what I am doing here?

You have just subconsciously applied everything learned in Strategies One through Six to this transition and are ready to problem solve. You are at a crossroads, and possibly the worst-case scenario for your transition. What do you do? Manageable parts! Remember, when we break things down into manageable parts, and address each part, then we are on the right track to success. This is how we utilize Strategy Seven and apply the four steps discussed earlier. This is how we apply the different problem-solving techniques to our transition. My wife constantly tells me I do not have plan A and B. I have plans A, B, C, and D. You must have options, so you can decide on the best course of action for your transition. Honestly, how can we truly know the right course of action or solution until we see what works and does not work? We do this through analysis and problem-solving; then we choose the appropriate response and apply it to the transition. We can perceive results, or guess, but until we apply the selected course of action we will not know the result. Most times, we apply our own knowledge or experiences to the course of action process, to help choose the best solution for the transition. This can be beneficial at times, but we need to remember to keep an open mind and to expand on what has been applied with Strategy Seven.

The problem with just applying what we are familiar with, and keeping a closed mind, is that we may not think about what can go wrong. The best solutions are those that are developed by looking at the best- and worst-case scenarios. If we prepare for the worst-case scenario, then we will be better suited to apply a problem-solving technique that is successful. Until we are in a position where we see what can happen, on all levels, we cannot be fully prepared for what comes. This is done to a point during Strategy Six, as we receive feedback on the inconsistencies observed during the evaluation. Strategy Seven builds on this, as it introduces the individual to worst-case scenarios, so they can see how to resolve the problem and expand on what we reviewed during the evaluation. Each solution is a scenario. Primarily, Strategy Seven looks to implement and develop new techniques for addressing the barriers or obstacles more effectively and efficiently through the use of problem-solving techniques and solutions.

The experience I want to share to help explain Strategy Seven is one that still affects me today. It involves events from my last deployment to Afghanistan, which was the most difficult. The evaluation I referenced during the discussion of Strategy Six provided me with the certification I needed to become a certified JTAC. I was certified to complete all aspects of my job and was ready for what came next. As I described at the end of Chapter Nine, I had recently transitioned into the Air National Guard and deployed to Iraq and Afghanistan as a certified JTAC. The deployment to Iraq was very rewarding and productive, but it was strictly an Operations Center based deployment, which means I did not leave the wire once. I was a certified JTAC but did not engage in any field time. The only aircraft controls I had were for training and observation from the Operations Center. The deployment to Afghanistan, which I volunteered for, was very different. Even from the start, heading into the country on the rotator, I had a feeling this would be different and something I would never forget. I felt prepared, as I had been a certified JTAC for over three years at that point, with numerous evaluations, controls and training under my belt. Don't get me wrong, I was not perfect; there is always room for improvement, but I felt ready for the challenge. I knew the tempo was high in the country and was excited to be able to do the job I signed up for, in the way I had always wanted: to test myself.

    I volunteered for the deployment with one of my good buddies from my unit. I was the JTAC, and he was originally coming as my ROMAD. We had volunteered as a team, and I was happy to be going with him. The problem was that he had just obtained his certification before we left and was very eager and ready to be a JTAC. We knew as we traveled overseas that they would most likely split us up for additional coverage as we were both certified controllers. After days of travel we arrived at our location in Afghanistan. We were there for about two minutes (not literally) before they told us they were splitting us up. He would be heading south to support operations there. After a few days, he was gone, and I was awaiting the arrival of my new ROMAD. I had volunteered for this deployment, so I was an augment, which meant I was filling a spot for an active duty unit. We were supporting the soldiers of the 10th Mountain Division of the US Army. My ROMAD arrived, and he was everything I thought he would be. Smart on the radios, young, cocky, and arrogant. It was like having a child at times, but all in all, he was a good dude, and we made a good team.

The tempo was high in that area during my deployment. We were a two-man team covering four companies, so it was busy. The terrain sucked, and we were always at a disadvantage, as the enemy always had the upper hand from the mountains. You would never know this by talking to my family; I never let them know what was going on. I would speak with them about once a week and always told them things were fine. This was definitely not the case, as each day you needed to prepare yourself that it might be your last. You never knew where it was coming from, and the unit I supported was constantly engaging with the enemy. It was tough. I controlled aircraft and directed air strikes from the Operations Center and the field daily, sometimes supporting troops that were a thousand meters away—but I could not see them because of the terrain. Additionally, the mountains of Afghanistan can reach about eight thousand meters (twenty-five thousand feet). Imagine traveling through this with about a hundred pounds on your back; it was like breathing through a straw. Not to mention the sweat rashes you would get from the rubbing and a temperature of over a hundred degrees.

This was very different from my previous deployments; I was truly doing the job of a TACP. The story I want to discuss in relation to Strategy Seven occurred about half way through my deployment. We were tasked with supporting a convoy heading to the Korangal Outpost in the Korangal Valley. Anyone who is familiar with the area and the many documentaries made on the war in Afghanistan is familiar with the Korangal Valley. It was nicknamed "The Valley of Death" by American forces due to the increased tempo and level of operations occurring there. The Korangal Valley skates the Pech River and is about six miles long and half a mile wide. It is surrounded by mountains with limited entry and exit routes, so I am sure you can imagine the levels of anxiety when traveling in and out to the Valley. My ROMAD and I had our own vehicle, and we were placed in the middle of the convoy. We lined up, checked communications, and headed out. There is more that goes into this, but all you need to know is that we were ready. I had submitted a request for air coverage and had a two-hour block approved to cover us on the first part of the route. It would be a long day of traveling before we reached our final point. The first leg of the convoy went smooth. I had good communication with the aircraft and company commander (who was in the lead vehicle). After a few hours, we hit the midpoint and stopped to refit and rest. I remember a bunch of us sitting around shooting the shit about life.

I met a female medic, who was about to move over to the Air Force because she wanted to become a nurse. She was excited about the move and looking forward to the transition. I met a young soldier who was about to get married. He was telling me that his fiancé was in the country a few hours away, and he would get to see her in a few days. I met a lot of good people, some just barely eighteen years old, who were deployed to Afghanistan for eighteen months, experiencing things that most people never will (or never should). At eighteen, I was drinking too much and partying, not fighting for this country. I give them a lot of credit and have a lot of respect for anybody who chooses to serve. So, the group of us sat and chatted and then prepped to head out. We lined up and started out. The aircraft I had requested had already busted their time, which meant they were out of fuel and headed back. I remained on frequency with the Operations Center to request immediate CAS in case we came into contact with the enemy. I remember hearing some soldiers talking before we took off, discussing how eighteen soldiers had been killed over the previous two weeks while traveling through the Korangal Valley. I will admit I was nervous but ready nonetheless. This is what I had been training for, preparing for, and I was ready for whatever came. Or at least that is what I thought.

The sun was shining. I could feel the heat of the sun on my face as we traveled through the Valley. I had opened the window to look around and see if I could observe anything in the mountains. I closed the window, took a sip of my hot lemon-lime Gatorade and chatted about some bullshit with my ROMAD, who was driving the vehicle. I had a headset on, which was linked to my radios, so my hands would be free if I needed to return fire. I remember conducting a radio check with my counterparts at the Operation Center, so communications, or "comms," were good. I began running through situations in my head, applying the concepts of Strategy Seven, problem-solving techniques, to different scenarios that could arise: worst-case scenarios. I did this frequently during my deployment, as you never know how to respond. I knew that I wouldn't know until it happened but wanted to be prepared to react. We continued down the road, if you want to call it a road, on our way through the Valley. That's when it happened. I can't even tell you what my initial reaction was, but I know my heart stopped for a second when I saw the explosion. The lead vehicle in the convoy was on fire. It appeared to have run over an IED, or Improvised Explosive Device. This was my interpretation from my training and past experiences in country, but it was the first time my convoy had ever been hit.

I didn't even hear the first bullet hit the side of the HUMVEE, but it was clear after about ten seconds we were being attacked from the mountains as well. I remember looking over at my ROMAD who was frozen, hands gripping the steering wheel, he looked terrified. I admit, I was scared—for about two seconds. I took a breath and remembered why I was there and told myself this was my job. I instructed him to get out and return fire, and I shouted over the radio, "Troops in Contact, Troops in Contact. Request immediate Close Air Support." There was more to it, but you get the idea. I opened the door and got out to return fire. As I opened the door, the company commander ran by me on fire. We patted him down to put it out, but he still wound up having about 10 percent burns on his body. I received word over the radio that I would be getting aircraft routed to my location, but it would take about fifteen minutes. This would be over in two minutes. The driver of the lead vehicle had been blown out the side and sent flying down the side of the mountain. The road we were on was narrow and was about fifteen to twenty feet from the bottom of the Valley. He managed to climb up to where our vehicle was located, and I will never forget seeing his face, covered in blood, at the driver side window, saying, "Help me, I am fucked up." We brought him around the front of the vehicle, to my side, where we were returning fire and using the rocks as cover. We couldn't see where anything was coming from. The enemy fire was sporadic and only lasted a few minutes. It was time for a SITREP, which is a situation report.

I was up on the radio, waiting for my aircraft. I remember looking for the medic I had met but couldn't find her. I watched an intelligence troop run across the road, then fall on the ground. He was frozen and unable to move. He was terrified. We helped him across the road and to cover. The gunfire stopped, and it was quiet. As I moved closer to the lead vehicle, I could see the young soldier I had chatted with earlier leaned up against the rock wall being attended to. I moved closer and could see he was in bad shape. As I continued toward him, I could see the life just drain out of him, and I actually watched him take his last breath. I remember, all I could think about in that moment was his fiancé. I helped lay him down as they placed him in a body bag. I remember still looking for the female medic and other soldiers I had met. I spoke with the company commander and informed him that the aircraft was on its way. He was getting his burns addressed and still commanding his troops. It was a crazy scene and my mind was all over the place. I finally spoke with someone who told me the female medic and gunner had also been killed. Their body bags were next to the young soldier who I had seen take his last breath. The sergeant I was speaking with said the gunners legs had been blown off and the female medic was decapitated. I had no words.

I could hear the crackle of the radio when the aircraft checked in. My heart jumped, as it was time to do my job. My mind was running, going through the different scenarios. I was in the worst-case scenario, and it was time to apply the different problem-solving techniques I needed to push through. My job was to provide air coverage, in any way I could, to cover and support my unit. That was my focus, and I began working through my processes, my transitions, and working to provide the most effective support I could, during an indescribable experience. In addition to aircraft overhead, I needed to coordinate the medevac helicopters to come in and ex-fill the wounded and killed in action. I spent the next ninety minutes controlling all aircraft overhead, de-conflicting altitudes, and making sure everyone was aware of the situation, while passing 9-lines to conduct Airstrikes for cover. Since we were in a troops in contact situation, we were a priority, and I continued to receive aircraft.

It would take a few days for EOD and the engineers to come out and retrieve the blown-up HUMVEE, so the fifteen of us remaining from the convoy would cover the position until reinforcements arrived and retrieved what they needed. For seventy-two hours, I communicated with the operations center, received constant air coverage, and conducted Airstrikes on the ridge lines to suppress the enemy from attacking again. Three days with no sleep or consistent breaks— constant support, and trust me, I was committed. I remember taking power naps in between missions, but I would jump up the second I heard the squelch break on the radio. We were all committed, and as the time went on and the adrenaline began to subside, the group began to lighten up and even laugh together. We were still ready for anything, but it was nice to begin to decompress what had happened.

I mention this because this is when I continued to apply the concepts associated with Strategy Seven on the obstacle we were facing, and think about the different problem-solving solutions I could apply. I had just experienced the worst-case scenario and pushed through the best way I could. I remember continuously thinking about ways I could have been better if this type of transition came again, and isn't that what we are meant to do? Succeed in our transitions. It's a process, and this was no different. I needed to trust the process and the men and women I served with, in case this happened again, because it could mean life or death.

Let me clarify something. I describe this story to show my experience and how Strategy Seven assisted me with moving through the transition. This by no means is meant to undermine any experience of other service members, or one-up anyone. Anyone who has served has their own experiences, own memories, and own scars. I have the utmost respect for all of them, and feel honored to call them my brothers and sisters in arms. Thank you for your service.

The rest of the deployment was busy, and the tempo remained high but nothing compared to what I had experienced that day. One thing I did know was that utilizing the concepts surrounding Strategy Seven and applying problem-solving techniques and solutions helped me move through the very tough transitions I experienced during that deployment. As you can see by this story, the solution is not always simple, and at times you will be required to think on your feet and apply problem-solving techniques in the moment. You can prepare for anything, but sometimes the solution is not clear until you are in the moment, and you have to be ready for anything, while trying to remain confident and positive. That is why it is so beneficial to apply the TLP to each transition. It prepares you to address anything that comes your way. Each strategy builds on each other and truly gives you the confidence, ability, and the knowledge, to overcome any obstacle and push through the transition—some scary, some happy, some sad, some memorable, and so on. They are all different, as our life is complex, but if we remain positive, and keep an open mind and healthy perspective, then anything is possible. The concepts associated with Strategies One through Seven prove this fact, as each provides its own manageable step in the process. Remember what I said in the beginning of the book—it's like a sports team. You're putting the best players together with one goal in mind, to succeed.

As has become a practice within this book, I ask you to reflect on the information provided and put yourself in a scenario where problem-solving techniques were either applied to your transition, or when you feel that if applied, would have helped you push through. Think about a time when you were required to make a choice in the moment, a time when you had no idea of the right choice or direction, a time when you were forced to select a solution or course of action when the outcome was unknown. Sounds familiar, right? We have all been there is some form or fashion, and we can all attest to the difficulties that come into play when we are unsure of the right choice. Applying problem solving techniques helps us through the process, and when added to the ideas behind Strategies One through Six, can ultimately maker our decision for us. It can help us decide on the best course of action, either in the moment or if we are able to prepare and plan for the worst-case scenario. Remember, we need to trust the process.

Now, let's look at it in this way. The players are the nucleus of the team right, but they do need help and guidance to succeed and complete the process of winning a championship. The same goes for the TLP and its strategies for success. Strategies One through Seven have a combination of internal and external factors for the individual to succeed and push through the transition. The common factor in the process is you, the individual. Strategy Eight, the last step in the process, looks at the numerous support systems available, and the ways you can round out the TLP by utilizing your performance support systems. Just as the players utilize their coaches, fans and management to succeed, it is important for you, as an individual, to utilize your performance support systems for success. We all need help at times, and as you can see from what has already been discussed. Even when we feel prepared, we still may need help and guidance. This will only increase our understanding and confidence, and ultimately, our opportunity to be successful. Strategy Eight is titled *Utilizing Performance Support Systems*, and it is the culminating point of the TLP.

CHAPTER ELEVEN

A Different Type of Transition Blanket

We all need help at times. This starts from the day we enter this world. We even need help out and into the world from the doctor and our mother. There are words of encouragement and even a push or two to help us enter our complex system of life. After the commotion settles (any parent who has been in the delivery room knows what I mean), we are wrapped in a transition blanket, a swaddle, and brought to our parents or nice warm bed. Of course, this is a metaphor I am referencing here, but Strategy Eight, the final strategy in the TLP, provides a different type of transition blanket. The premise behind it is similar, as it is meant to help us transition and feel supported. Strategy Eight utilizes performance support systems to help conclude the process. The primary goal of this strategy is to reinforce the abilities both developed and uncovered during the execution of Strategies One through Seven by utilizing the many performance support systems available to us in order to complete the transition process. Up to this point, we have worked through the transition and exhausted all that each strategy entails, but now it is time to reinforce our thinking by utilizing the support systems available to us.

The intriguing thing about support systems is that they can truly reference any system which we can tap into to help us succeed. They are meant to reinforce what we have developed to this point, whether it is an emotional system, physical system, mental system, mechanical system, etc. Remember, our life is a complex system and support systems work as a subsystem so to speak, as they are meant to assist in our success and ultimately help us be better and to help us power through the transition. To this point, we have been inundated with new knowledge, examples, visual aids, practice, feedback, evaluation, and problem-solving techniques to help us transition through the process we are working through. The final strategy, also an external factor, is solely based on someone or something outside of ourselves. It enlists the support, help, or assistance of a third party to bring the process full circle. Remember, there is no finish point with transitional learning. It is continuous, circular, and you can reattack any strategy at any point to help you succeed. Tell me that doesn't sound good. A process that will not judge us, tell us what is right or wrong, and that is always there to help and make us better. I would sign off on that!

Even when we are prepared, we still may have questions or want to check ourselves. This is required within continuous learning, because the second we think we know everything, is the second we stop learning. So even when we feel prepared, maybe because we put a lot of hard work and time in, it still feels good to check our work and/or our ability to be successful. This is where support systems come into play. Think about a study group or tutoring session. They don't do the work for us but guide us and help us to be better at whatever we are attempting. Especially when we encounter obstacles and barriers, because sometimes, it gives us the guidance we need to push through the transition and increase our level of confidence. We all need help sometimes, and this different type of transition blanket is a very beneficial resource towards success.

Just as each transition is specific to the obstacle or barrier you may be facing, so are the support systems needed to help you through each process. You wouldn't ask advice about cooking if you were looking to increase your understanding of philosophy. This may seem unrelated, but the point I am making is that if you are utilizing a support system, you need to choose a path which can reinforce your process for the transition you are addressing at that time.

One of the most beneficial aspects of Strategy Eight is that you can use the information obtained from the support system to enhance your own processes and tools. As a child, our brains act as a sponge and pick up most everything we encounter. We are always learning and utilize the enormous amount of support systems at our disposal for advancement. As we grow, our levels of knowledge and understanding expand, so this process changes, but we are still able to obtain new knowledge and comprehension from the many avenues and resources we are exposed to. As we utilize our performance support systems, we can recreate our own processes for future use. This is an enormously beneficial tool. If applied correctly, it truly supports the ideas applied during the previous seven strategies. We can go back to prior points in the process, adjust where needed, and build on what we are working on. As long as the framework is solid, which is the positive outlook on the new information, then the sky's the limit for everything after that. Think about the possibilities here. If we maintain this positive perspective and work through the different strategies within the process, re-attacking where needed, we can use our support systems to reinforce these ideas and ultimately make us better.

You can never have too much support, at least in my opinion. I have learned in my lifetime that the more we utilize our support systems, the higher our chances are for success. Each time we utilize support, we build on the framework we have established with the new information. Every transition starts a new process in our complex system of life. If our framework is grounded and strong, applying support will only make it stronger. Support systems are like the support beams of a house. It just reinforces the strength of the framework. Support systems can also challenge us to be better within ourselves. If we see something that exceeds our current abilities, or that could make us better, we want to apply it to our own transitional process. Remember, it is OK to ask for help, to be humble and admit we do not know everything, and that we may need someone or something to help us exceed our capabilities. There is nothing wrong with it, as it will only help us grow when we use the resources at our disposal to be better, to ultimately succeed.

Support systems vary, some work for us and some don't. It is never a bad practice to apply support systems, even if they don't wind up working for the transition it is being applied to. You will only know if you try, and it is up to you to decide what works for you and your transition. This is why it is so beneficial to create new tools and processes within the transition if possible, because it makes the most out of the resource and support system being utilized. There is nothing wrong with being afraid or nervous, and this should not stop you from moving forward. Fear is only a state of mind, and can be viewed in a positive way to assist with your process if you let it. If we let the unknown drive our thoughts and emotions, we are already behind the power curve. It's why the Law of Attraction is so amazing to me. Its concept states that whatever we put into the universe is what we will get back. Our life is a reflection of our thoughts and emotions, and this idea cannot be more correct within the TLP.

Fear can be scary. Sounds funny to say, right? But the truth is, fear is scary and when we give into fear, we are already giving up in a way. If we give in to fear, we are not living up to our full potential and letting the fear about what we think is going to happen control our decision. I bring this up because there are numerous support systems available to assist you through the transition process, to include times when fear may play a significant role in your decisions. Think about a time when fear played a role—when you let fear win and control your decision. Think about a time when you let the fear of the unknown tell you how to react.

Now, think about the support systems available to you during that transition. Did you utilize them? Did you apply them? Did you even know they were available? We have all been there and have made choices that helped our transition, but also choices that didn't. I want you to think about how different these choices would be if you applied the Eight Strategies for Success to that transition. I have found when we look at things positively and utilize the support systems at our disposal, the fear tends to lessen and even disappear at times. I still experience fear. It is inevitable in my opinion, but it's what you do with that fear that makes the difference. The examples I have discussed to this point started when I was a child and continued through adulthood. Each transition has built on one another and made me better for the next. The experience I want to use to help describe the impact of Strategy Eight reinforces this idea—as each experience has prepared me for the greatest gift I could ask for. That gift is becoming a father. Any parent can relate, and we all know support is a much-needed resource when you have a child.

I will never forget the day I found out I was going to be a father. My wife and I were so excited, and I will admit, I was terrified. I was ready and couldn't wait, but just as many first-time fathers do, I wondered if I would be a good dad. I lost my father when I was twenty-four, so I did not have a support system in place to guide me on becoming a father (from a father's perspective that is). All I knew was the type of dad he was, and I only hoped I was half as good as him. What I did have was my wife, and honestly, I could not have done it without her. My wife is a strong, independent person, who will tell you EXACTLY how she feels. It is one of the reasons I fell in love with her. One thing I can say about my wife is that in many ways, she is the smartest and most talented person I know. Her ability to control a room and a conversation and make people smile is pretty special, and it is how we found common ground early in our relationship.

Another thing is that my wife is the epitome of a self-made person. She is not perfect, as none of us are, but she has fought to become the amazing woman and mother she is, and I have more respect and appreciation for what she has accomplished in her life, and brought to my life, than I can explain in words. My wife has been a mother since she was twenty-one years old. I will not tell you her age, but we are close, and she constantly reminds me that I am older than her. She has a lot of experience being a mother—and a pretty amazing mother at that. So when we found out she was pregnant, I immediately knew that she would be my primary support system, and I couldn't have felt more comfortable. Thank you, babe, for all the support you have provided me and our kids; we are all better for it. My stepkids are seventeen and nineteen and our boys are five and eight, so there's a lot more support to go, but I can honestly, and with a full heart, say part of the father and man I am today is because of her, and the support and guidance she has provided me, and continues to provide me, when I need it the most. You still amaze me every day, and I love you more for the person you are and continue to become. I love you, Colon (not her real name). Now, let's wipe our eyes and discuss how Strategy Eight fits in.

I began making lists of what to do from the time we found out (because I am a planner). I am famous for my lists and folders, but, hey, shouldn't we always be prepared? We began the journey and started looking at houses, found out the sex, started buying baby items, discussed names, and so on. The name came pretty quickly and easily, so we checked that off. Over the next eight months we started getting ready and preparing. I was like a fish out of water and looked to her for guidance. I read all the baby books and asked her all types of questions. She was very patient with me and helped me to see all the different aspects of becoming a parent, with the primary goal of being successful throughout the transition. This was the most important transition I would ever encounter, and because of who and how I am, I wanted to do everything I could to be ready for whatever came my way—including getting my wife anything she craved and needed. I was very attentive to her needs, and (lucky for me) her vice was cereal. Pretty easy right. All I have to say is Batman, babe, remember Batman and his sidekick Robin. I will leave it at that.

Picture this setting: my wife is a week away from giving birth, and we are moving into our first, recently-purchased house together. Talk about stress. She took it like a champ, and we made it work and were ready for the arrival of our new addition. My wife had a scheduled cesarean birth for our first son, so we knew exactly when he was coming. I remember lying in bed the night before talking about what was coming. We were so excited. We shared this moment, laughed, cried, and felt amazing—until we heard my stepson scream out, "Mom, Sis keeps making me smell her finger." Got to love kids.

We woke up and headed to the hospital. There are no words to describe how I felt; it was surreal. But, I admit, I was nervous. In our usual fashion, we joked and made light of the situation, as we do, and my beautiful son was born and a member of this world. I remember holding him, looking down at his face and feeling like I just won the lottery. I was a father, and I was going to be the best father I could be. But, I knew I needed help. The next few weeks were going to be an adjustment. I had no idea what was in store for me, but I was ready because of the support system I knew I had. I am a very involved father, and both of my boys know that Daddy is always there if they need me. I make it a point to be that way, and it started from the second my oldest was born. Lucky for me, my oldest son was an angel. He slept through the night, adjusted through his transitions quickly, and was a really good baby. My wife reassured me this was not normal, and we should feel lucky. My boys are pretty amazing, and I treasure being a dad. This started with my oldest son's birth. I feel like the luckiest dad in the world, and this continued when we had our second son. One funny thing about my oldest is that he has crystal blue eyes. The only person in either of our families who had blue eyes was my dad, so we know he is looking down on us and watching over our kids.

The next two years after having my oldest son was a learning period for me. I was working through my transitions of being a father, and a primary success strategy for me was utilizing the support system in my wife. She helped me with so many aspects of being a parent, so when it was time to start planning for our second child, I felt like a pro. Well, as any parent can tell you, they are all different and bring different experiences, and my second son was no exception. We started trying around October, and my wife got pregnant in about three seconds. I remember coming home from work one day, and she had a small box and card waiting for me. I opened it, and it was a positive pregnancy test. We smiled, hugged each other, and started crying. The preparation would start again. I felt more confident this time around, but my wife continued to tell me that it would be different. Just another example of her support and guidance. In my eyes, it would be the same and just as easy. If it wasn't for her, I would not have been prepared to the level I was without utilizing my support system. I prepared just as much for my second child. Maybe I prepared more—going to all the appointments, buying baby items (at least the ones we couldn't reuse), finding out the sex, thinking about names, etc. The name took a little longer this time, but again, it was no question once we realized it. We were having another boy, and I couldn't wait.

The experience was different this time. We had our two-year-old and had to explain things to him. This added to the preparation, and my wife helped with the different ways to do that so he would feel happy about having a new little brother. I love to read, as I have discussed before. Since my boys were born, I have read to them or with them every day. It is a special time for me with them, and we all enjoy it—well, most of the time. So when my wife recommended those big-brother books, it was a no brainer. We read them with our son, and he was super excited for the arrival of his brother. My wife was a champ throughout the pregnancy once again, and again, her cravings were not bad. They could usually be quenched with a delicious french dip (of course with au jus on the side).

I was so excited for this new addition to our family and to become a father again. I read even more books and prepared as much as I could, utilizing my support system to the best of my ability. We were ready.

Again, my wife would have a cesarean birth, so we planned the day and got everything ready. We went to the hospital and fell right into our old routine, laughing, joking, and being us. The time came, and my wife did amazing. I will never forget the nurse handing me my son and looking down being amazed at how I was lucky enough to feel this feeling again. I felt like I had just won the lottery a second time. After the commotion settled, and we were in the recovery room together, holding our child, I remember looking at my wife and just feeling like I was on a cloud. I transitioned and was now a father again. Just like before, right? Well, at least that's what I thought at the moment. I would soon find out that was not the case.

The nurses informed me and my wife that my son was having some breathing issues, and he needed to be placed in the NICU for observation. His lungs were not expanding the way they wanted, so they needed to observe him. My heart dropped, and I felt like I was not ready for this. My wife felt the same, and we both needed each other to work through the transition. To make matters worse, my wife had just had surgery, so she was not allowed to go to the NICU to be with him. Just imagine how that would feel as a mother; I remember feeling so terrible for her. Fortunately, I was able to go down to the NICU to be with him. I brought my older son, and the three of us hung out together and took photos for mommy. I will never forget the feeling of helplessness I had, seeing him lying there hooked up to all of the machines. I was so happy to be his dad but terrified for him at the same time. It is a feeling I do not wish on anyone, and still, I tried to remain positive. My older son and I fed him and took photos with him, and I held him as much as possible. I knew this was torture for my wife, so I wanted to make sure she knew we were with him. It was one of the hardest things I have ever had to bear in my life, and we were very lucky that he pushed through and was cleared to leave the NICU to come up to the room with my wife and our family.

Remember how I told you my wife will tell you EXACTLY how she feels. Well, the nurses figured that out pretty quickly. After about a day, my wife made sure it was clear that my son would be brought up to her or she would be down in the NICU. That day, my son was cleared to leave the NICU and brought up to her room. It was a sense of relief that I still think about when I look at him, and I am just so thankful that he was and is OK. My boys are everything to me, and I couldn't imagine life without them. They are both amazing in their own way and both have very different personalities. As with most children, one is more like me and one is more like my wife but both share some pretty amazing commonalities, and I am so very proud of them. They are both sweet and caring, smart, thoughtful, and love to laugh. They are well behaved (at least with other people) and are respectful and loving boys. It is so amazing watching them grow, and I feel so proud to be their dad. I am very proud of the boys they are, and a large part of it is because of the support systems available to them. As their dad, I try to be patient and understanding, calm and compassionate, and do things in the best way possible. No one is perfect, and they are little boys, so I am sure you can understand that they test the boundaries on many levels. Parenting does not have a playbook; there is no clear answer on how to do it, even with support. I have had to accept this fact at many points. It has made me a better father, husband and man, and I would not change my journey for anything.

My wife was not kidding. My second son was very different from my first. He was not difficult by any means, and I was definitely more prepared, but he was definitely a different baby then my oldest. I loved it though, just as I did the first time around. I worked through each transition to the best of my ability and utilized the support system I had in place, and it is a process I will never forget. My boys are five and eight now, and I learn from them just as much as I teach them every day. I am so proud of them and tell them constantly—as long as they try their best, I will always be proud of what they accomplish.

The TLP process is not foolproof by any means. It's a process, and by applying the strategies outlined in this book, it can assist in your success. It is still up to you to push through each transition and live up to your full potential. Remember what I asked earlier: what is perfection and success, anyway? If you are living up to your full potential, isn't that success? That is what the TLP does. It uses the strategies for success to build on your abilities and help you live up to your full potential in a positive and confident way. I have provided examples from childhood to fatherhood; the strategies can be beneficial throughout your many transitions. As you can see by my experiences, some examples are happy, some sad, some tragic, and some humorous. I have tried to portray the fact that it is a process, and within our complex system of life, we will go through many different transitions with different experiences and outcomes. The goal is to remain positive and push forward. That is why the TLP is so beneficial; it is successful when you work through the process and live up to your potential. If we break things down into manageable steps, anything is possible. Nothing is guaranteed in this complex system of life, and as you can see by my examples, we can prepare all we want, but it does not mean things will end up exactly how we want. The strategies for success just help us achieve our full potential and give us a better chance to end up where we want.

In a way, I have lived a lifetime in my forty-one years to this point and have achieved and accomplished things that I never thought possible. I am not bragging by any means, just making the point that if we work hard, push ourselves, and trust the process, odds are the outcome will be where we want it to be. If not, we keep trying until it does. We will hit barriers and obstacles along the way—it is inevitable, but that's when we need to dig in and press. Now that the Eight Strategies for Success have been laid out, and you can see how success is possible, it is time to discuss some not-so-positive aspects associated with the process and your transitions. Every process can have a presence of negativity associated with it. What matters is whether we give in to that side of the process and focus on the barriers and obstacles facing the transition, or if we perservere and push through. The next chapter goes over how the TLP can assist with overcoming these obstacles and build on positivity.

CHAPTER TWELVE

The Bumps are What We Climb On

By this point, you have seen how the Eight Strategies for Success can be applied to the different transitions within our complex system of life and be successful. As I have continued through my life, I have encountered many transitions where the different aspects of each strategy have been applied, but that doesn't mean it came without struggles, barriers, or obstacles. Barriers exist, but what can make the process positive is that we can build on the barrier and push forward instead of defaulting when our mindset (our cognitive approach to the situation) is positive. The bumps are what we climb on to be better, as it's not a matter of getting knocked down, it's whether or not we get up. More importantly, it's what we do when we get up that can make all the difference. No matter how hard we try, there will always be difficult times. I have provided a few experiences from my complex system, but difficult times exist just as much (and maybe even more) than the good times. It's about perseverance and about pushing forward because the bumps are what we climb on to reach the summit or peak of our potential. The next two chapters are dedicated to the bumps in our life—first the bumps we encounter in the professional and academic setting, and then the bumps we encounter in everyday life. The focus is on the presence of barriers and obstacles in our complex system and, more importantly, how the different strategies within the TLP can assist with overcoming these barriers.

Remember the reference to the crossroads point in your journey, earlier in the book? We all have choices, and we all have the choice of which direction we choose to go. Sometimes these choices will work out, and sometimes they won't. The benefit of this is that our choices are infinite, as our ability to make a choice will never go away. We always have an option, and the ability to make a choice. I am not saying these choices will be the right ones all the time, but just as we can circle back within the TLP, we can do the same with our choices. It is our choice to give in to the barrier or overcome it. Remember, fear can be a good thing at times; it can keep you on task and ready for anything. It's the way you perceive fear, react to it, and apply it to your transition that makes the difference. I hope by this point, as I have provided personal details associated with my complex system, you can see how fear and perseverance have played a role in my life. School, work, and everyday life is the trifecta utilized for this book, with the primary goal of showing how the strategies within the TLP can be applied and ultimately be successful to all aspects of life. Remember, this is a self-help book, not a textbook, so the goal is to teach through relatable scenarios—ways of helping you see the strategies and their components in play. Trust the process!

What constitutes a bump in the road? There is no clear and concise answer for this. Bumps, obstacles, and barriers mean different things to each of us and represent different transitions. The commonality rests with the term *transition*—bringing us from one point to another. Many of the examples I have described focus a good amount on positive reactions to each transition when applying the Eight Strategies within the TLP. The next two chapters will discuss examples where I needed to get up and fight to better myself—first with work and school, then in my everyday life. The trifecta is different for everyone, but this is what it means to me.

I will never forget when I received the news from my college that I would be placed on academic probation. I was shocked. I don't know why I was shocked, I mean, what do you expect is going to happen when you go to five classes during a semester? Seriously, I literally went to five of my geology classes during the spring semester of freshman year. I had made it through my freshman year but was sitting at a whopping 1.79 GPA and was placed on academic probation. I needed to obtain a 2.5 my first semester as a sophomore or I would be academically dismissed from the school. I was attending SUNY Cortland in upstate New York, and even though I was loving the social aspects of life, I was not putting the same amount of time and dedication to my studies. Hindsight is twenty-twenty, right? If I had known then what I know now, it would be more like foresight is twenty-twenty, which ironically enough is the title of this book.

I started the beginning of my sophomore year with a positive outlook, but I was already behind the power curve; I was still trying to figure out shortcuts to get me to the 2.5 I needed to continue at school. I took classes that I felt I could pass with no problem, including the infamous Introduction to Management class discussed earlier in this book. I registered for the minimum amount of classes required for full-time students (four) and believed I could get Bs and Cs with little to no effort. That would get me to the next semester. I began the journey in the wrong mindset; I was not looking to apply my full potential but just enough to pass. This was not going to cut it, and I soon found that out. I crawled through the semester giving somewhat of an effort, which meant I was not attending just five classes, but I was not taking advantage of all my opportunities for success, or applying any of the strategies for success and their underlying concepts. The result was what you would expect.

My father knew what was needed, and he knew the exact day we could call the school for the semester grades before they came in the mail. I remember not being worried but—in the back of my mind—kind of knowing the result would not be where it needed to be. We called the number together, and the person on the other end said, "2.3 GPA." I will never forget the look on my father's face, because it wasn't anger—it was pure and simple disappointment. My heart dropped, and we stood there in silence for a second. See, I was the first one in our immediate family to go to college. My godmother had attended college, but other than her, I was the first. My dad worked hard to pay for it, and I just simply let him down. The feeling I had in that instant will live with me until the day I die. Even the person on the other end told my dad that if I would have just retaken the courses I failed from the prior semester, then it would have given me what I needed. There was a chance I could get another semester if I spoke with the dean, but my father was not having it. He said, "You made your bed; you lie in it and fight your way back."

My only option was to go to a community college for a semester, obtain a 3.0, have a meeting with the dean, and then I would be eligible to return to school if she let me back in. So, I began looking into my options. At home in Staten Island there were not many options for me. I looked in Manhattan and Long Island, but they were not an option because it was too late to register. My only option was to go back to Cortland and go to the community college in the next town. There were guys in my fraternity in the same boat, so it made sense (at least in my mind). Nope, another bad decision. My father agreed because it was my only option, and he told me that this was it, and he was not paying for it. If I did not get back in after the semester, I was out. Not just out of school but out of the house. I agreed and headed back. Long story short, I partied, drank too much, hung out, and went to school when I felt like it. Even worse, I gave up halfway through the semester and stopped going altogether. When the semester ended, my father looked at me in disbelief and just shook his head. Did I mention I didn't tell him I had stopped going? When my report card came in with all Fs, the choice was already made. I was out. Even then, I tried making excuses and acted like I didn't care (I did by the way). I was forced to move to California and live with my mother. Fortunately, my stepfather got me a good job at the hotel where he worked, and I said I would go back to school later. It took about three seconds working full time at twenty to realize just how good I'd had it and what I'd thrown away. This is when I approached the wall and saw no way around the obstacle. I was stuck and full of regret.

I was still in contact with people back at college. I visited school a few times and vowed I would get back there as a student. I felt like I was missing out on so much, but mostly, I felt like a failure. My father would not even let me come visit his house until I got my shit together, so that's just what I did. I made a choice to change directions and turn my transition into a positive one. I made a choice to climb over the bump and persevere for the better. Remember the notorious notes I told you I would write my dad? Well, he received one in the mail from me shortly after this decision. I asked his forgiveness and told him I was going back to the community college and would be readmitted to my original college. I asked—if I was able to get back in—could I come home? My father called me shortly after and told me that if I proved myself, then he would consider it. He said he had lost faith in me and that hurt more than anything.

On the next trip to visit my college friends, I registered at the community college again and started planning my return. Once I returned to work after that last trip to school, and after I had registered for the upcoming semester, my mindset had changed. This transition occurred in both my academic and professional system. I was placed on the night shift at the hotel and began preparing for my return to school. I had about six weeks until the next semester was starting and needed to save as much money as I could. My outlook was more positive, as I had a plan and felt like I was on a path towards success. I saved every penny from work, stopped going out all the time, and sold any of the items I did not need anymore. My goal was laid out, and I knew what I needed to do to obtain it. The transition was a combination of academic and professional goals, since one affected the other. My focus had to be on my success and what I was looking to accomplish. Once I did that, the choice was easy, and the barrier did not seem like such an obstacle. I did not feel stuck and began pushing harder and harder towards my goal. I was ready to succeed, and it all started with making the right choice, for me, and living up to my potential.

Let's review the Eight Strategies for Success and their components. I would receive the new information, relate and recall examples, integrate visual aids, practice, institute feedback, take tests, apply problem-solving techniques, and utilize my support systems. The barrier I was facing within my transition was to be readmitted to my original college and, in the interim, regain my father's respect. I would look at returning to school in a positive way—not focusing on what had happened but what was to come. I would think about ways that I was successful and relate those examples to my goal. I would integrate text or illustrations to help me understand the information, study, and practice, take tests and assessments, and receive feedback and results. Finally, to help me succeed, I would apply problem-solving techniques and think about worst-cases scenarios, utilizing all support systems and resources at my disposal. I would trust the process and the strategies for success!

I returned to school a few days before the semester began and made a deal with one of my fraternity brothers to use his car two days a week to attend class. What I was missing before was motivation and the reality of what I was expected to do, and ultimately what I needed to do. It's different for everyone, and for me, it took consequences as major as failing out, my dad's disappointment, and the reality of what I had given up to show me what I had done and how to make the changes I needed to make. I needed to view my transition in a positive way and make all the aspects of my goal work for me. Remember, part of the process is to make the different strategies work for your specific situation, so the solution becomes obvious and attainable. Manageable steps, right? I set my schedule to attend classes on Tuesdays and Thursdays between 11:30 a.m. and 4:30 p.m. and one class on Wednesday from 4:00 p.m. to 6:30 pm. I was going to class Tuesdays through Thursdays, and never before 11:30. This gave me four days between classes to get work done. I also had time between classes at school. I changed my mindset about school as well. I focused on classes and what I was required to do—very different from before. I must say, I surprised myself at times, and it only increased my levels of confidence. At the end of the semester, I logged into the school website and saw my GPA: 3.25. I did it and even exceeded my own expectation of a 3.0 GPA.

It was so clear to me at this point. It's crazy how one choice, one transition, one goal, can change your mindset and thinking about things. After I had failed out and disappointed my dad, I felt very similar to the way I felt when I lived at my mother's in high school. I felt defeated, weak, and not good enough. I felt very discouraged and like I was nothing. Remember, it is not about getting knocked down, it's about whether you get up—or not—and what you do when you get up. For a good bit after I had failed out and moved away, I felt lost. I tried to tell myself I was happy and doing well, but I was just lying to myself and not being truthful to who I was at that time in my life. It's all about perception, and I was trying to perceive my actions in a positive way, but it was not realistic and deep down I knew it. The truth is, I had lost my confidence and was not being true to myself and how I was feeling. My choices after I had failed affected not only my relationship with myself but the people around me—people who were counting on me to live up to my end of the bargain. I let down my family, friends, and most importantly my dad who had worked hard to give me something he never had.

No matter how much I tried, I was unable to truly accept what I was doing. I was not being truthful to myself or who I was and needed to be. This is the opposite of what is required by the strategies of success associated with the TLP, since positivity, confidence, and determination are embedded into the process. We need to push forward and climb on the bumps in order to be better and succeed. It is the only way we truly live up to our full potential and our abilities. We can reattack the different sequential strategies if need be, but the second we choose to stop moving, continuously learning, and trusting the process, then we have already lost and given up. Success is possible and for the taking. It is up to us to make our own fate and make it happen, and even though there are external factors available to us and support systems in place, it is still up to us to use them and keep pushing forward.

As you can see by the bumps provided in my complex system and this particular story, it is very easy to get discouraged and give up. Sometimes it even feels like the right thing to do, as it is easier, sometimes, than pushing forward. There is a line from *A League of Their Own* that makes me think about this. It's a great movie, and my wife and I reference it frequently every time we sing to each other. There is a scene with Tom Hanks talking to Geena Davis about her quitting. She told him that it just got too hard. Hanks looks at her and says, "It is hard. The hard is what makes it great." This could not be more correct. Life is full of bumps and difficult times when it feels like we are defeated and want to give up and like all we can do is give up. But the truth is—that is just a choice. Life is full of choices and if we break them into manageable parts, anything is possible. This is the case when it comes to obstacles or barriers. Sometimes we can do it alone, sometimes we need help, and sometimes it takes more than one attempt, but if we remain positive and keep pushing and, working hard—then anything is possible. Success is possible if we trust the process.

I did two things immediately after getting my grades. I scheduled a meeting with the dean at SUNY Cortland, and I called my dad. He was proud of me and said to come home for a visit soon and we would discuss the next steps. I felt pretty good at this point and felt like I had climbed over the bump or barrier in front of me with success. There was still a lot to get through, but I was happy with the direction I was going. I had the meeting with the dean a few days later and was admitted back into school on a probationary basis. I needed to obtain a 2.5 GPA the next semester at SUNY Cortland and then I would be fully readmitted. Déjà vu, huh? It was solely up to me, and I felt ready and like I knew what I wanted, at least I thought I had it all figured out. I was so excited and locked in a ride to go visit my dad a few weeks later.

During that break, before I went home, I had a lot of down time. It was summer, and I was not doing anything. I played video games, hung out, and watched a lot of movies. I watched *G.I. Jane* a bunch. After watching it a few times, I began thinking about joining the military. Funny, I had seen so many military movies in the past. Just as most people my age, when I watched *Top Gun* for the first time, I wanted to be a fighter pilot. I thought about the military when I was sixteen and we went to my brother's Parris Island Marine Corp graduation but that was about it. I took the Armed Services Vocational Aptitude Battery (ASVAB) test during my brief stint living in California and even entered the Delayed Entry Program (DEP) but quickly changed my mind. I remember not feeling fully invested in any of it, like it was just a thought. It still makes me laugh to think how much watching *G.I. Jane* in May of 2000 made a difference in my life and my plans for the future. I still can't explain it, but it triggered something.

I was readmitted to SUNY Cortland at this point on a conditional basis and started looking into the different reserve corps for the military. I had a buddy in the National Guard, so knew I could go to school still and be in the military. My fraternity brothers found my newfound path humorous, especially what brought me there (G.I. Jane). A different recruiter was coming to the house every few days to meet with me. I met with all the recruiters and decided that if I was going to do it, I would join the US Air Force Reserves. I spoke with the recruiter and let him know my plans. I had already taken the ASVAB when I was in California, so all he needed to do was request everything, and then I would choose a job. It took a little bit for him to obtain everything from the Military Entrance Processing Station (MEPS) in California. That worked out great for me. It gave me time to really think about it, and I was going to see my dad soon, so this was something else we could discuss.

I was still on the fence at that point but was leaning toward doing it. It was just the reserves, right? I could still go to school and would only have to do one weekend a month (two weeks a year) but still serve. Yeah, I didn't know anything really and was kind of driving blind, but it seemed like a good idea, and something was pulling me in that direction. The Law of Attraction is a powerful thing and all signs were telling me to do it. It was another transition and barrier—one that was focused more on life itself and the direction and choices in my life. The next chapter will go into this aspect of applying the TLP strategies to barriers and obstacles in everyday life and the choices we make in life. It is meant to show how beneficial these choices can be when the strategies for success are applied to our transitions. The summer of 2000 was one I will never forget. It was the first summer of the millennium—the first summer I was twenty-one years old and of age to drink. It was also the summer where a single decision in my complex system of life would change the direction of my life forever.

CHAPTER THIRTEEN

Life is Like a Road...To Anywhere

Do you ever find yourself driving down a road, lost in thought, until you realize you missed your turn or found yourself off track? I am sure this has happened too many of us at different points in our lives during the different transitions we encounter. Our minds are constantly preoccupied with other things, and we tend to lose focus when we are overwhelmed. Life can be like a road—a road to anywhere we choose. It's full of twists and turns, bumps and barriers, flat ground, it brings us places we choose to be—or do not choose to be—sometimes. Sometimes the directions we have or lay out are correct and sometimes they are not. The trip seems easy to navigate—until we are completely lost and have no sense of direction. The weather and environmental conditions cooperate, and it is sunny and beautiful, but sometimes we can barely see in front of us and need help navigating to our destination. Life has a starting point and an end point, not to be too morbid, but we will all leave this life one day—just as, during a journey, there are transition points, intersections, and times when we have to divert or change course. The only common ground is the fact that there is a starting and end point, but what we do in the middle, during our journey, is what can make all the difference.

Choices. We all have them. Good choices, bad choices, our choices, other people's choices, etc. Choices will always exist, and it is up to us to make the right choice for our specific journey. I wish I could tell you that every choice will be successful or easy, but it will not. This is a self-help book, but it's not fiction. Success comes from failure or a loss just as much as it comes from winning (maybe even more at times). We all fail, and sometimes we need to fail in order to see the right choice and act on it. We are all different, and the different transitions we encounter in life are what guide us through these choices. We may be given a task or destination we are required to get to, but it is up to us on how to get there. If I have learned anything in my complex system to this point, it is that the road is not always what it seems; it is not always laid out, and you do not always end up where you expect. Life is hard, and we all have our own struggles, barriers, and obstacles. You have gotten to know me throughout this book and been exposed to some of the challenges and successes I have faced and overcame, but we all have them, and it is up to us to make the right decisions for our own complex system of life. The right choices through each transition will help us succeed and reach our destination on time.

I like analogies and metaphors. I feel they help see the point and more importantly, relate to the information (as in Strategy Two). The TLP is not perfect, it does not guarantee success in everything; it's a tool that, when applied correctly and to each transition in a way that benefits the individual, will increase your chances for success. Remember, success is not always clear; it does not always show itself in the most understandable ways. It takes many forms and, as discussed earlier, can come from failure just as much as from winning (or what we perceive as winning). The TLP helps us break things into manageable steps, utilizing each strategy to work through the transitions, obstacles, and barriers that come along with them. Let's look back at the road analogy. The TLP is like a map for the complex system of life; each strategy is a destination. Each destination will get you closer and closer to your final goal. Think about how good we feel when we are lost but then figure out a route that works. As we get closer and closer, we feel better and better, and this positivity only increases our chances for success.

When I was in technical school for the military, there was a field portion we were required to complete. This is our "field week," so to speak. It tests our endurance, knowledge, and ability under pressure and stress, giving us the opportunity to see what we are made of. Now, I am by no means comparing this to any other service or training, as the TACP training has its own barriers and obstacles, including the field portion of the training. The reason I bring this up is because one of the training requirements we are expected to accomplish is foot navigation. We complete a practice route with an instructor and then a practice route on our own. On the third day we complete a final navigation and are evaluated. We need to complete both a day and night navigation course in a specified period of time by ourselves. If we fail, we are given one chance to retest the following day, and if we again fail to meet the requirement, we are recycled and have to complete the block of study all over again. We are tested in many ways during the week, in ways like sleep deprivation and being "smoked," which means we are required to complete physical training requirements in full gear and beyond exhaustion. The wooded area surrounding the base is pretty rough—you can get caught up frequently. The brush (the field conditions of the surrounding foliage) was beyond difficult. I completed the day navigation with no issues, and then it was time for the night navigation. I was ready for my evaluation.

Have you ever tried walking through the woods with eighty pounds on your back in the pitch-black dark with nothing but a compass and small red light to help you? Not very easy, especially for a kid from NYC. You are required to plan your navigation with a map, set your route, and execute within the required time period. I utilized all of my training, prepared, and headed out. I knew my start and end point, and planned the route. I wish it was that easy. Each transition brought on its own challenges, including literally getting wrapped up in brush; I had to cut myself out. I pushed forward, though, diverting and utilizing the training when needed. I am happy to say, I made it to my point with time to spare and will never forget the feeling of joy when I called in over the radio and was told I completed the course and to wait for my ride. I did it, but it did not come without its own challenges, changes and adjustments, and feelings of negativity, wondering if I was going to make it.

This experience and the previous chapter discuss transitions with work and school. The new experience for this chapter focuses on the final leg of the trifecta previously discussed, the transitions we see in everyday life when we are required to make choices at the different transition points in our life—times that can change the direction of our complex system, which may completely change our course. As discussed at the end of the previous chapter, I had just gotten back into my university and was speaking with reserve recruiters about possibly joining. I was about to head home to visit with my dad and discuss my options. This is where the implementation of the components of the strategies for success played a distinct impact in my life, my road or direction—a transition that would change my life forever. It's crazy when I think about it now—where I was in my mindset and thinking and the direction I believed was my chosen path in my complex system of life. Little did I know that one decision would change everything for me and help me succeed in a way I never thought possible. It all stemmed from one decision—a thought and a choice in a split second, changing my route and direction. Even my dad didn't see it coming. It was solely my decision and one that I would not change for anything in the world. I was scared, nervous, and unsure, but I was also excited and ready. I keep thinking about the movie *G.I. Jane*; it sparked an interest for me—one that grew into something I can't even explain in words.

I remember driving back from Cortland to Staten Island with my friend. He was going to drop me off in Staten Island before heading to Long Island. We enjoyed a few road sodas on the car ride (yes, very bad idea), and I felt good about where I was in my thinking. He dropped me off around six in the evening and I had dinner with my dad and stepmom. It was mostly small talk; the detailed conversation would come the next day. My room had already been converted into a guest room, and it was occupied by another family member, so I slept in the basement on the pullout couch. We had a nice, finished basement so I didn't mind, but I remember laying there thinking about how I screwed everything up. The next morning, I woke up, and my dad and I had a very long and detailed conversation. He reiterated how proud of me he was but still did not feel comfortable letting me move back in because what was to say I would not do it again? I can't blame him, but it still hurt. I would say what hurt the most was that my dad lost all faith in me, and he wasn't the kind of guy to just give it back. I told him I understood and then told him about the reserve recruiters and what I was thinking. I could see the shock in his face but also the happiness that came along with it. He smirked and said, "Wow, didn't expect that." He told me he thought it was a good idea and that if I joined the reserves I could move back in the house and use his address as my home of residence. I remember tearing up and thanking him. Deep down I knew this was something I needed to do. Now, this may seem like the transition point where applying the TLP and its strategies helped me succeed, but it wasn't. There is even more to the story.

I settled back home and contacted the USAF reserve recruiter. I informed him of my decision, and he started the process. I let him know I needed to be back in time for the following spring semester. He followed up with me about ten days later and told me I was set to leave in August. I would do basic training and then technical school, and I'd be home in November in time to go back to school in January for the spring semester. The college was also fine with my decision, and they changed my re-admittance to the following spring semester. I had told the recruiter I wanted to leave ASAP, so he got me in the first available job: health care administration (adminitrative airmen who work in the clinic). I didn't care; I just wanted to serve, to go, and get back for school. I was all set with my route planned and feeling confident and like everything was in place. Yeah, not really. There was still something inside of me that was holding me back, a feeling I could not explain. I just didn't feel fulfilled, like I still was not living up to my full potential. To everyone else, it all seemed great. The school was happy, my dad and family were happy, and my friends were happy because I would be going back to school the following semester. Something just seemed off. It took a stop on the road to help me see where I needed to go—a choice during a transition that was clear as day—an epiphany so to speak.

It was just after the Fourth of July and my dad and stepmom would be going to California on vacation for a week. They would leave me home to take care of the house while they were gone (my stepbrother lived in Manhattan by this point). I was about four weeks from leaving for basic training, due to leave the first week of August. I took them to the airport and would pick them up the following Tuesday night. I remember leaving the airport and thinking how nice it was to have things set up. Being twenty-one years old, with the house to myself and my parents gone, my immediate thought was, "Yes, a party." I would have my friends over that weekend and we would rage. I spent the next two days preparing things, and on Friday night, friends from high school and college made their way to Staten Island and to my house. There were about twenty-five people there, and we had a blast. Grilling, drinking, and bullshitting to all hours of the night. It was fun, but I had no prior approval of it from my dad and deep down I knew I probably shouldn't have done it, or at least I should have asked permission. When I woke up the next morning, Saturday morning, most of the people crashed at my house. No one drove home who was drinking, so a good number of people were still there. So, we decided to keep it going. We partied all day again and into the night. There were fewer people at my house Sunday morning but still a good number. It took about half the day to get everyone up and out, but by about 1:00 p.m., it was just me and the dog. I had a pug named Bill, and I think he even looked at me in disgust. My friends tried to clean up, but I am sure you can imagine what it looked like when a bunch of hung over twenty-one-year-olds try to clean up. The house was still a wreck.

I spent the rest of that day cleaning and even knew I would be cleaning on Monday as well. My stepmom liked things a certain way, and I needed to make sure it looked perfect. The transition point I want to mention, about how the strategies for success can change your direction, occurred during this time. I will never forget it. It was a split-second decision, but its effects changed my life forever. I remember sweeping up, thinking about what had happened. I started thinking about college, failing out, getting back in, the reserves, my dad, etc. I remember thinking, "I am still drinking and partying six nights a week." Would that change when I got back to school? Maybe I should go into the active duty USAF and attempt school when I was at a more stable point in my life? I started applying all of the strategies for success to this barrier—this transition point of what was best for my life. For about two hours I processed the information and recalled and related examples of the thought of going into active duty. I integrated visuals aids by looking up the active duty USAF on the Internet. I applied Strategy Four by simulating what my life would be like if I went back to school, or went into the active duty USAF. I evaluated myself and my abilities, if I could change when I went back to school, and reflecting on if I would make it. After I finished cleaning, I jumped on the infamous AOL chat rooms (remember, it was 2000), and I chatted with and received feedback from people in Air Force in the many chat rooms. Over dinner, I started applying problem solving techniques and worst-case scenario situations to the transition. What would be the worst that could happen? I worked through the transition process, and the answer was clear. Why was I going back to school? Why was I putting myself back in a situation where I knew I would probably fall back into the old routine? Why was I not living up to my full potential? The answer was so simple and a wave of clarity came over me. I needed to contact an active duty recruiter and go into the active duty USAF and not the reserves.

I can still feel the weight being lifted; the answer was so clear, the transition was so obvious, and my confidence in the decision was beyond what I could have imagined or portrayed in words. So, I applied the concepts associated with the final strategy for success within the TLP, Strategy Eight—support systems. That night (Sunday night) I sent an e-mail to the active duty recruiter explaining my situation. I followed up on the email the next day and spoke with him on the phone. He was very receptive, and as I was already through the MEPS process, so he just needed to switch me to active duty and secure a job for me. We began the process, and I could not wait to tell my dad what was going on when I picked him up the next day. The reserve recruiter was not so happy and tried to get me to change my mind. I informed him I felt confident in this decision and appreciated all his hard work. I picked my dad and stepmom up on Tuesday night wearing the Air Force T-shirt I got from the reserve recruiter. I informed them of my decision on the ride home, and my dad was absolutely shocked. He actually did not think it was the best idea at first, since he wanted me to go back to college. When we got home, he immediately asked me if I had people over. How the hell did he know? I had spent two days cleaning. I should have known, though. I went to a Catholic high school, and in the two years living with my dad, I cut school exactly one time. He must have known because he came home early from work that day to find me sitting on the couch watching television. Yeah, no getting around it, I was caught.

I proceeded to come clean about the party and tell my dad about everything that went on. I could see his face change throughout the discussion, and honestly, I could see the pride in his face—not because I was going active duty, I later found out. It was because I was truly growing up and made a decision that I knew would not be easy but that needed to happen to better my life. I could see the pride in his eyes, and that meant more to me than anything. For the next week, I worked with the recruiter to get everything set and ready. I didn't know anything about active duty, so I trusted him. He told me that my best bet would be to go in as Open-General, and I could leave in three weeks and have any job in the Air Force I wanted. Yeah, not true at all, but what did I know? I was set to leave at the end of August for active duty, and I was so excited. You know from previous chapters that I doubted the decision later, but ultimately, I pushed through and made my life and career what it is today.

Before leaving for basic training, I went back up to school on opening weekend with a friend to visit and let everyone know I would not be coming back. My friends were bummed, but understood, and we had a great weekend. I will never forget driving home with one of my best friends who had also decided to leave the school. He chose to attend a different school. He turned to me in the car and said how much respect he had for my decision and thought it was a good idea. It felt good, I have to say. The night before I had to go to MEPS to ship out, my dad and I went to the diner for dinner, and then a movie. That was our thing, movies. Mets games and movies, but movies all the time. We saw *Hollow Man* and had a great conversation over dinner. He told me how proud of me he was, how scared for me he was, but how much he respected my decision and was excited for what was to come. I couldn't hold back the tears. We hugged, and all the tension, disappointment, and regret began to fade away. All because of a choice—a transition point where I remained positive and made a specific choice for my journey. The next day after work my dad dropped me at the recruiter's office, hugged me (cried a bit) and told me he was there if I needed him and to do my best and live up to my full potential. I was ready and felt very confident in what was next. At the end of basic training, my dad surprised me when he came to my graduation. I already knew my mom was coming, so it was nice having both my parents there for this transition, as it truly changed my life forever.

That was August of 2000. Since then, I have served on active duty, in the Air National Guard and Air Force Reserves. I have been to war on three separate occasions, lived all over the world (including Europe), traveled to places I never thought possible, and met all different types of people, some of whom I still speak with today. My career and education have thrived due to my military service, helping me through the many different transitions in my complex system of life. Have there been bumps? Absolutely. At times I doubted myself and wondered what was next, but I pushed through, and the military has helped me with these decisions a great deal. One decision, one choice—and my life changed in a way that I never thought possible. It changed in a way that I will be happy to share with my boys one day. So they can see we all have choices, and when we work hard to our full potential, who knows where the journey will go. In my case, it led me to the man, the husband, and the father I am now, and I couldn't be more thankful.

This was my process, my choice, and how I applied the TLP strategies for success to a transition which changed my life. My journey. Life's journey looks different to all of us, but if we trust the process, remain confident and positive, and apply the TLP strategies for success to the different transitions in our life, our own personal success is there for the taking. Success is what you say it is, and only you know what works for you, what is meant for you, and what helps you live to your full potential. Trust the process and it will guide you on the road of life, as it can take you anywhere.

CHAPTER FOURTEEN

Next Stop...

Life is a journey. As we discussed in the last chapter, it's like a road with numerous transition points, stops, diverts, etc. We don't always know the route, but we all know there is a starting point and an endpoint. The route is not always laid out for us and needs adjusting at times, but we can be sure of a start and end point. Now, some people may see this as a bad thing. Some people like to have everything laid out and explained because it brings comfort. This can be beneficial and feel secure but can't it also make you feel like you may be missing something—missing an aspect of the journey that brings risk, excitement, and intrigue? Part of the intrigue and joy in our complex system of life comes from the not knowing and the unexpected.

Think about the experiences I have presented to this point. The aspects of my life where I did not know what was going to happen next. Yes, sometimes it brings sadness and disappointment, this is a part of life, but it also has brought happiness, extreme satisfaction, and success! There have been times when working hard and pushing through has made the difference, and the outcome has been positive and successful. This is the journey I am referring too.

Have you ever been on a long-distance train ride? Think about what you saw on the journey. You know, where you were starting from and where you are ending. The route did not change, but what you saw on the way was new, exciting, and had the ability to change the way you looked at things, maybe sparking an interest in something you never thought possible. The last chapter talked about a road and the obstacles and barriers you may hit along the way—but how your life can change by pushing through and applying the different strategies of success to overcome them. This chapter focuses on what you may see along the journey, and how continuous learning and applying the strategies for success will only enhance your experiences. I remember the first time I took a long train ride. I was twelve years old, and my brother and I were going to see my mother for Christmas. My mother was living in Pennsylvania, so my mom and dad communicated (rare for them), and decided my brother and I would take the train together to see her. There were no train changes, so all we needed to do was get on the train and my mom would be waiting on the other side. I was twelve and my brother was fifteen, so it was not a big deal for us to be alone. My father watched us as the train left the station and we were off.

I remember I was excited—mainly for the journey and what I would experience. This was something I had never done before, and I was so excited about not knowing what was next. I remember looking out the window, watching and observing, seeing just how different the world was. I was excited for the food cart and snacks as well, and I remember how my brother let me sit by the window. I put my headphones on and pushed play on my Diskman (remember those?). I was ready for anything, but I had no idea where the next stop was. The unknown can be a scary thing, but it can also be an exciting aspect of life. It will test us and our abilities. It's really up to us and how we choose to both view and experience the journey. It's up to us whether we want to look out the window and experience change or look down and just take the ride.

Learning is continuous, and the second we choose to stop learning is the second we give in or give up (in a way, that is). I tell my boys all the time—no one knows everything, you can always learn more. Our journey starts and ends but the train ride we experience, or roads we take, are only avenues for the journey. They are the vehicles that provide us with a way to transition, but all of the tools, resources, and aspects we use within the journey are up to us. The TLP and Eight Strategies for Success are associated with both internal and external factors, utilizing numerous support systems and our own abilities for success. It may require attacking a transition numerous times to accomplish the goal intended, and you may fail before you are successful. Remember, success is what you say it is, not the other way around.

One aspect we have not really discussed yet, which is vital for success in anything we do, is trust. Trust can be a difficult thing; it can be scary for someone who has had negative experiences with trust to fully embrace the idea. I have lost trust in my life—both in the people around me and myself at times. You have read many of the instances in my life where trust and confidence were a problem but also that I challenged myself to move past the obstacle and continue learning. It was just part of my journey, and it's just another transition point in the complex system of life.

The TLP strategies for success actually rely on continuous learning, as success within the transition starts with positivity, trust and confidence. Trust in yourself and the people around you. The key is to keep moving, observing, learning and being excited about where the next stop is, just like we experience during a train ride. I have shared a great deal of transitions in this book—primarily to help you see where the TLP strategies for success can be applied and be successful, but ultimately, to help you relate to the barriers we face throughout our transitions. We all encounter different transitions on our journey—some you may be familiar with and some you may not. I am sure everyone reading this can relate to something presented within the Eight Strategies, as the aspects explained with each are things many people experience in some way or another during their journey. This chapter is about continuous learning and how—if we continuously apply the TLP strategies for success to the different transitions in our life—success is possible. Remember, success is what we say it is, and it is different for each individual during each person's journey.

There are two recent transitions in my life that I am very proud of—transitions where continuous learning and applying the TLP strategies for success are vital to my expected outcomes. My first try at college was not very successful. My focus was on other things, and it took me many failures to figure out the right path for me. When I failed out of college at age twenty and could see the disappointment in my dad's eyes, I vowed to make it right. The journey or path in regards to my education was just beginning, and I was not going to give up that easily. I vowed I would fix it and make my dad proud. It was nothing he said to me or made me feel, it was just something I knew I needed to do. I told myself at twenty years old, I would go all the way. I would complete my associate's degree, my bachelor's degree, a master's degree, and ultimately a doctorate. I was twenty, and I had no clue what the journey would look like, but I knew where I would ultimately end up—where it said on the train ticket.

After joining the military, I started working toward my goal. My job became very busy as deployments started, even when I transitioned into the Air National Guard. No matter what came my way, I continued taking classes and kept pushing. While on active duty, I took a few classes towards my associate's degree, but it wasn't until I entered the Air National Guard that my education became my primary goal. I remained positive and continuously took classes, anyway that I could. I was enrolled at SUNY Old Westbury in a Bachelor of Arts program for Sociology, which was my primary path. The issue was I was deploying and traveling for work a lot, so I started taking classes online as well. I did this, continuously, from 2005-2011, when I eventually graduated from SUNY College at Old Westbury with my BA in Sociology. In May 2011, at the age of thirty-one, I did it. I completed my primary goal by remaining positive, confident, and trusting my abilities and the people around me.

I then took a job in Sacramento, California working for the military and moved my whole life from coast to coast. After settling in, it was time to continue with my education and start the next part of my journey: my master's degree. I began taking courses for an MA in International Relations, and after two and a half years I accomplished the goal and obtained my degree. During that time, I got married, had my first son, and started building a life with my family. It was not easy, but I stayed on track and continued learning during each transition. To me, the outcome was successful when I was awarded the degree. Remember the diversions and obstacles we discussed earlier? Well, my life, my journey, and my path was no different. After completing my MA degree, I was informed the contract I was working on with the military would be ending. What was I going to do? I had a family to support. I remained positive and started looking into my options. This was just a barrier, a transition, and I would trust in the process, in myself, and in the people around me.

A large part of my job as a contractor was to teach. I loved it! I enjoy being in front of people, as I am sure you can recall from the Introduction to Management presentation story. I enjoyed it, and I was told I was good at it. Teaching has always been something I have been drawn to, and something I was hoping to continue to do as an adjunct professor one day. So, I started looking into teacher certification programs. I utilized the numerous support systems available to me and found an accelerated hybrid program with the University of the Pacific. It was a year-long program, nine months of coursework and three months of student teaching. This was perfect! My contract would end right around the time I needed to student teach, and it would be a smooth transition (so I thought). I began the program and worked through each transition the best I could. The diversion came when I was about a month away from finishing the course requirements. My family is and always will be the primary concern of my life. Making sure they are taken care of is everything to me, so as I always do, I had plans B, C, and D on deck. I had applied for a more secure, permanent, government job during this time, which is different from contracting. I interviewed and found out about a month prior to my contract ending that I had been offered the job. It was decision time.

After weighing out all the options, it was clear the best route for me to take was the one that would help me support my family, and provide me with the opportunities I always wanted for my professional career. I chose the government job, and (just about six years in now) I am so glad I did. I have transitioned into different positions within the agency during that time but am so thankful to all I have worked with—my current supervisor knows I love coming to work every day. Once I decided not to complete the certification aspect of the program, the University of the Pacific gave me the option to complete a thesis in order to graduate. I completed the requirements and graduated with an MA in Curriculum, and Instruction. It was now on to the third aspect of my plan, the doctorate degree.

As I was working full time and in the career field (government service) that I wanted to be in, I needed to choose the right fit for my doctorate. I am very thankful for my career and have been working in government service, both as a civilian and in the military, for my entire adult professional life—more than half my life span actually. In addition, one of my goals was to teach at the college level one day. My MA was education based, so I started looking into the different programs available to me in the field of education—but that I could utilize in my current position. I started comparing PhD programs to professional doctorate programs. Professional doctorate programs are geared toward working professionals, and it seemed like the better choice for me. I found an EdD program, which is a doctorate of education degree, in PI leadership that I could complete online. This was it! A combination of education and leadership courses that would help me reach my goal. So, I began taking courses in 2015.

It took me five years to complete. It was not easy, and there were many early days and late nights, but in June of 2020, my degree was conferred. I was a doctor of education. I could not have done it without remaining positive and staying on my path. More importantly, I could not have done it without the support of my wife and kids, as they helped me in ways that words will not explain. This is where I created the TLP strategies for success, during my capstone project for the degree. The hope is that this book, future books, and teaching will help to show how continuous learning applies and can help you be successful. It took me twenty-one years to get to my goal, but I did it. A large part of my journey is dedicated to my dad; I know I let him down after my first attempt, so I am hoping he is looking down on me with a big smile on his face and his forehead shining, knowing that I did it all in part for him. I hope I finally made him proud. It is also for my boys, so they can see that anything is possible as long as you work hard and try your best. That is all I will ever ask from my boys, and I will be proud of them no matter what they choose to do. I bring this up not to brag or gloat but simply to show what hard work and continuous learning, in conjunction with the concepts associated with the TLP strategies for success, can bring when applied to your complex system of life. That is, your own personal success, as we each have a different journey.

Now, they say work should be fun, right? My chosen profession, government service, is my path for security. It provides the security in life for me and my family and I enjoy serving. We also need hobbies, side hustles, or other areas where we can thrive and be successful. Taking risks and pushing forward are items associated with continuous learning, and this next example is nothing shy of that. This is a recent transition that started as a "nothing to lose" scenario with some really good friends—brothers, more like it. Three of my best friends and I recently started a production company. We have no experience in the business, but are ready, willing, and excited about what it can bring. We are ready to succeed and utilize the support systems and resources around us to be successful. This is an idea we have been talking about for over twenty years, starting after we left college. The idea began as a movie but over the last two years has evolved into a television series that focuses on four friends from Staten Island, who attend college in upstate New York. They are thrown into a world they are unfamiliar with and all it entails. The premise is set in the late '90s and brings everything the late '90s had to offer. It paints a picture of college in the '90s that has not been portrayed, including life as a college student attached to an unsanctioned fraternity, and I have to say, the final product has turned out pretty amazing.

I mentioned the show's website (www.cowbirds.com) earlier in the book; we are still in process of creating this future masterpiece. I bring this up because without continuous learning, we would not be where we are—currently ready to pitch it and wait for its success. My partners of Buddy Buddy Productions, LLC, are all in with this project, and we even began working on future projects. We continue to utilize all aspects of continuous learning to better understand the business and what is needed for success, appling the strategies for success to the different transitions associated with the project and our company. My business partners are some of the smartest guys I know, and we make each other better. Remember, positivity is the key to success, and we all remain confident and dedicated, continuously learning with each step of the transition. We consistently say, it's not a matter of if—just a matter of when—this and future projects will get picked up. We are all excited about what is to come but creating this and working on the project together has also helped us remain close and in touch, building on our relationships and support systems. I couldn't ask for better business partners and can't wait for the red carpet and Emmy nomination one day (we can hope, right?). I am sure my buddy Leo is currently doing the hands, Frank is looking for FDT's next big move, and Rob is sleeping. All kidding aside, I love these guys like family and am better for knowing them.

Continuous learning was the focus of this chapter and its experiences. It is the culmination of what the TLP strategies for success has to offer, and I hope these experiences show how the strategies for success can be applied and how continuous learning is present within the process. The train ride will end at some point, but it is what we do during the journey that matters. Success is for the taking, sometimes it is right in front of us, and sometimes we need to find it. Taking risks is not always a bad thing, and as you can see by the many experiences provided in this book, when we remain positive and push through each transition, success is possible. Trust the process. Anything is possible if we break things down into manageable parts, and the TLP strategies for success can help to address the obstacles and barriers we encounter during each transition. We each have a story and a journey, encountering transitions that are easy and hard. The process works if we let it. I hope each and every one of you enjoyed what this book brings, but more importantly, what the TLP strategies of success can bring to your own life. You just have to let it!

Next stop....who knows? But isn't that the way you want it sometimes?

CONCLUSION

Life is not easy. We each encounter obstacles and barriers each day that make us who we are and fill our lives with all different emotions. The TLP strategies for success are meant to assist us with navigating the different transitions we face in our complex systems of life, while remaining confident and positive, and working toward our goal of success. I mean, these are strategies for success, right? The contents of this book are meant to show some of the different forms of transition we face and how if we apply each strategy in the correct and proper manner, success is possible. I have mentioned this over and over in this book and can't say it enough: trust the process and it will bring positive results. I truly mean every word of this, and I want to end this book with an experience that has been the hardest transition I have ever encountered. My current situation.

As I hope you can tell, my family is everything to me. I am a very involved husband and parent and do everything I can for my family. I have been in the military for about twenty years at this point and have been on numerous deployments. All of my prior deployments to combat zones were well before I had a family, so it was just me to worry about. I had no ties and was able to focus on my job and what I needed to do with no distractions. I thought my last deployment to Afghanistan would be my final one, but I was wrong. I changed military careers about seven years ago, shortly after my first son was born. Put aside that my body was not cooperating anymore, I did not want to be away from my family if a deployment came up again. It was time to transition, and I was ok with it. So I found a position that satisfied what I wanted for my military career and still let me serve. The last seven years in my second Air Force Specialty Code (AFSC) has been very rewarding. I have met and worked with some amazing people, and I can honestly say my current superintendent is the best boss I have ever had in the military. I thought deployments were in the past for me, but last year, in the beginning of 2020, I found out I would be deploying again for six months in 2021.

Due to privacy concerns, I will leave the particulars out, but I knew I would be deploying and away from my wife and two young boys, away from my family. As I said, I am a very involved dad, and my boys are used to me being with them every day. My boys would be without their dad, and I would be without them. My wife and I both had our struggles growing up and know how important it is for a child to have both their parents. Also, I believe marriage and parenting is a team effort, and my wife and I attack all aspects of our boy's life together—Team Warner, as we have come to call it. So when I was told a year prior that I would be deploying it was a shock. You know, you can try and prepare for it, but in the end, there is no preparing. I would be away for six months and that was that. Everything at home would be on my wife's shoulders and even though she is the toughest and most capable person I know, it's a lot to have to deal with alone. More importantly, my wife and I are best friends and truly look forward to the end of the day together. There is nothing I can say to describe how hard we knew it would be. Like I said, it is the hardest transition I would ever have to make.

Fortunately, the particulars of the deployment were probably the best they could be for a deployment. They are able to come visit me, and we get to talk and FaceTime numerous times a day. Again, it is not easy or the same by any means, but at least I get to see them every six to seven weeks, and talk to them every day. My wife and I love our shows together and part of our decompression time is to sit down after the boys go to bed and watch a show together. It's our routine, and we look forward to it every day; we get to be together and relax. While deployed, we have continued the tradition and try daily to watch a show together before bed over the phone. It's not the same, but it helps. I play toys with my boys over Facetime, we read books, do homework, and laugh and dance, just as we do at home. Again, it is not the same, but we make the best of it. Being away from them all is the hardest transition I have ever been through in my life, and I say this in real time, as I am currently writing this book from my deployment.

This is why I bring this up: the TLP and its strategies for success are helping me work through this transition with success and a positive outlook. Instead of sitting by, I chose to push through the obstacle and persevere. I decided to write a book, continue with military professional development, continue working on side projects like Cowbirds and Running Lowe (our new and exciting idea), and remain positive. I set a goal to read one book a week, and I am on track with that. I started meditating and reading the Bible—ultimately, to remain positive and push forward. This is my journey, my choice, and I choose to remain positive and succeed.

I can honestly say that this is the hardest thing I have ever been through, and I miss them every second of every day. I wish I could just hug and kiss them and tell them I will be home soon after every call, as I constantly feel the void of being from them every day. They have come to see me twice already and the scene in the airport was like something right out of a movie. The reason I bring all of this up is not to end this book on a sad note but on a positive and motivating level. Even at the hardest points in our life, when things are nowhere close to where we want them to be, being positive will help us succeed and push through. The bumps are what we climb on, and obstacles and barriers are forever present, but if we choose to remain positive, confident and persevere, then success is possible and for the taking. It may not always be ideal, or how we see it, but it is there and is always attainable. Our journey dictates the path, but we choose how to accomplish it.

I chose to take everything I have learned, experienced, and been through in my life and write a book that shows how, when we remain positive, and apply the strategies for success to each transition, success is possible and the outcome will be beneficial to our complex system of life. My family and I are working through this transition together. Some days are harder than others but we work through it together. This is our support system, and we apply the ideas present in the strategies for success to working through the obstacles and barriers so the outcome will be positive. The key is that we do it together and each work through our transitions to the best of our ability, living up to our own individual potential. I hope this book shows everyone reading it, including my children, that foresight can be twenty-twenty, and if we remain positive, confident, and always live up to our own potential, anything is possible if we work hard and persevere. Odds are in our favor that we will be successful in our attempts to overcome adversity and push through the different transitions we encounter in our complex systems of life.

I hope the TLP strategies for success, ideas, and concepts presented in this book help you push through the obstacles and barriers you encounter in your own complex system of life, just as they have helped me in mine. Remember to always trust the process and break things into manageable parts. More importantly, be positive and remain confident in your abilities, trust in yourself and your potential. It's all a process and success is there—you just have to take it. Live up to your potential and you will always succeed. Success is what you make it, and it is up to you how hard you try. Now, go apply what you learned here to your next transition. I can't wait to see what happens. Don't forget, it's not a matter of if—it's a matter of when. Good luck in all your future endeavors...and remember, foresight is twenty-twenty. Trust the process and you will succeed!

NOW IT'S YOUR TURN

Discover the EXACT 3-step blueprint you need to become a bestselling author in as little as 3 months.

Self-Publishing School helped me, and now I want them to help you with this FREE resource to begin outlining your book!

Even if you're busy, bad at writing, or don't know where to start, you CAN write a bestseller and build your best life.

With tools and experience across a variety of niches and professions, Self-Publishing School is the only resource you need to take your book to the finish line!

DON'T WAIT
Say "YES" to becoming a bestseller:

https://self-publishingschool.com/friend/

Follow the steps on the page to get a FREE resource to get started on your book and unlock a discount to get started with Self-Publishing School

ABOUT THE AUTHOR

Michael Warner has over twenty years of experience working in the field of training, development, and instruction. He has spent his entire career working in public service as a civilian and as a member of the United States Air Force. Michael has earned both a master's degree and a doctoral degree in education, specializing in performance improvement and development and is the founder and CEO of Summit Performance Solutions, LLC. When he is not writing or serving his country, Michael enjoys reading, watching sports, exercising, traveling, and spending as much time as possible with his family. His family means everything to him, and his accomplishments are just as much theirs as his own. He resides in Sacramento, CA with his beautiful wife and two amazing boys. For more information about Michael, visit www.summitperformancesolutionsllc.com

www.ingramcontent.com/pod-product-compliance
Lightning Source LLC
Chambersburg PA
CBHW072149100526
44589CB00015B/2152